The DESIGN& PRINTING BUYER'S *Survival Guide*

DON SPARKMAN

Allworth Press, New York

Published by Allworth Press, an imprint of Allworth Communications, Inc.
10 East 23rd Street, New York, NY 10010

Library of Congress Catalog Number:
ISBN: 1-880559-28-5

Designed by Sparkman + Associates, Inc.

To those who had to learn these lessons
the hard way.

CONTENTS

7   **Introduction**

     History

13   Graphic Design Then and Now

19   Typography, Prepress, and Printing Then and Now

     Graphic Design

27   How to Qualify Graphic Designers

39   How to Buy Illustration and Photography

45   How to Proofread Like a Pro

53   How the New Electronic Design Technology can Help You

63   How to Write an Effective Design Bid Request

     Prepress & Printing

71   How to Select a Printer

77   How to Select Printing Papers

87   How to Write an Effective Printing Bid Request and
     Purchase Order

Managing Your Department/Promoting Your Company

97 How to Set up a Charge-back System

103 How to Create a Graphic Standards Program

111 How to Effectively Promote Your Company

Terms and Trade Customs

123 Business Terms Commonly Used

131 Graphic Arts Terms Commonly Used

153 The Graphic Design Trade Customs

171 The Printing Industry Trade Customs

Appendix

181 Professional Organizations and Publications
     That Can Help You

191 References and Selected Readings

193 **About the Author**

195 **Index**

INTRODUCTION

There are many "How To" books on the various facets of the graphic arts. There is the International Paper Company's *Pocket Pal,* a necessity for anyone serious about a career in the graphic arts. There are many technical books on the market about the business of design, prepress technologies, and printing methods. These books are written for the people working in those fields, not the buyers of those services.

The Design & Printing Buyer's Survival Guide is not a technical handbook. It does contain some technical information, but only enough to let you understand the processes. This book is a serious look at the business of buying graphic arts products and services. This guide is filled with lessons learned the hard way, through experience.

Recently, my studio completed a direct mail piece for a national association. My designer specified a premium recycled sheet. The following week the client called my designer and told her that the printer had touble running the sheet and had to use another stock, thus making her job a day late. My reaction was not to blame the sheet of paper. It was a number-one grade and I had samples of other jobs printed on that same paper. What made more sense was that the printer had a problem meeting my client's deadline and used the paper as an excuse. I told the client that instead of not using that sheet again, I would recommend not using that printer again. This is the kind of situation that you will come across everyday and that's the reason for this book.

I'm sure you've heard of the "School of Hard Knocks." This is about the school of hard business. Common sense is the thread binding these pages together. Unfortunately, anything connected to the arts has a way becoming subjective. This is why you must be the level-headed member of the group.

...do not leave this book on your desk. Hide it. Who needs to know how you got so smart.

If you buy graphic design, typography, prepress services, paper, or printing, you will learn how to get the most for your company's dollar. There are ways of turning low budgets into highly successful projects. There are tricks known by the pros that can make you look like a hero. And let's face it, you don't need many mistakes to become a corporate loser.

Whether you work for an advertising agency, a commercial organization, a non-profit institution, city or state government, or for yourself, the rules are the same. It is unusual, in the current economy, for anyone to be able to buy with total freedom. Bids are the rule, no longer the exception. In the past, buyers could sole-source their work. That meant you could have a favorite vendor, and simply send your work to them and receive a bill later.

Survival is an art. Why leave it to chance? Mistakes are

made when common sense is not an important part of the buying process. There are many mistakes made daily, and you can profit from them. Many of them were also made in the past, and are discussed in this book. Last but not least, do not leave this book on your desk. Hide it. Who needs to know how you got so smart?

HISTORY

We've come a very *long* way, in a very *short* time.

CHAPTER 1

GRAPHIC DESIGN THEN AND NOW

S ince most companies have people on staff capable of writing, graphic design is usually the starting point in the graphic arts process. To understand graphic design today, we need to know a little about the recent developments in the field. I'm not going to take you back to the days of cave drawings, and I'm not going to bore you with a lesson in art history.

The Early Years

In the first half of the twentieth century, commercial artists/graphic designers were primarily typesetters and printers. Some were illustrators but they were totally different from people who designed pages. Until sometime in the 1950s, graphic design was little more than an embellishment of the printed word. There were pockets of where design mattered, but I'm talking about the mainstream. Examples can be seen in the old stationer's books, which gave the buyers of printing strict and rigid formats for their letterheads, envelopes, and business cards.

In the early part of this century, advertising design and illustration lived a separate life from graphic design. Advertising agencies used wonderful illustrations, hand lettering, and creative borders to sell everything from underwear to fine cars. What set the two industries apart? Money. For most companies, corporate identity was not even a glimmer in someone's eye. Design seemed frivolous and was considered by most within the business community to be an unnecessary expense.

The Beginnings of an Industry

Let's look at the sixties. Things were changing. A few true graphic design firms were starting to spring up in the metropolitan areas around the country. These companies were primarily in New York, Chicago, Dallas, Houston, Los Angeles, and San Francisco.

The typical scenario in 1966 went something like this: A printing salesman (never a woman) would visit his favorite graphic design firm. The salesman would present his customer's requirements to the designer. The designer would produce a hand-crafted layout in pastels or markers and explain, to the printing salesman, the rationale behind the graphic solution or layout. The designer would take the layout and put it in a plain envelope. The printing salesman would then affix his company's label to it, and go to his client's office. This worked well for a while. Graphic design appeared to be an in-house function of the printer.

As more and more design firms cropped up, the corporate buyer became more sophisticated. Good graphics were emerging everywhere. When the buyer felt the design did not suit his needs, it was rejected. This put the printing salesman in the position of having to return to the designer with a rejected layout. The designer may have followed the printing salesman's instructions to the letter, but the instructions may not have been an exact interpretation of what the buyer wanted. Something as simple as the client's disliking the color could cause a layout to be rejected.

When it became apparent that the designer had to be paid for a good faith effort when the buyer refused to accept the work, the printing salesman began to question his role as a broker in this new era of graphic design. It wasn't long before the printer introduced the designer to the client. The designer agreed to protect the printer's interests while working directly with the client. This took the liability away from the printer and thus graphic design became an industry. And a growing industry at that.

Yellow Submarine Era

In the 1970s, "corporate identity" made its major debut. There were companies who had developed strong identities much, much earlier. But for the most part, they were the elite. They were the AT&Ts, IBMs and GMs of the country. In the seventies, every company felt it had to have a corporate identity.

This was called the "Yellow Submarine" era of graphic design. Push Pin Studios, Milton Glaser and Seymour Chwast were the renaissance men of design. Other greats like Massimo Vignelli of Unimark, Paul Rand of Westinghouse, Saul Bass, and many others made the late sixties and seventies a highly charged time for the graphic design industry. The Beatles introduced the music that set the stage for this exciting time. Whether you loved or hated the seventies, they changed our lives forever.

The Business of Design

While the look of graphic design was changing, so was the business of graphic design. Graphic design firms were brokers for the most part. That is, they would buy typography from a typesetter and bill their client, adding a handling charge, based on a percentage of the actual cost This was called a mark-up. Design firms would often buy the printing for a project, and mark it up as well. All in all, this was a very lucrative way of doing business.

The shoe was now on the other foot. The printer's customer was now the designer. This lasted well into the eighties, when the nation's economy was heated up. Some design firms even got into the typesetting business, and bought expensive equipment. Every angle of making money was explored by the graphic design industry.

Unfortunately, what goes up must come down. Clients with great track records and proven credit were suddenly going out of business or, at the least, turning into slow payers. The designers were often left with the big bills from the printers and typesetters. Brokering was dangerous for small design firms without much working capital behind them. There is no insurance sold that will protect against failing clients.

Design Joins Technology

Meanwhile, in the late 1980s, computers were introduced to graphic designers. There were a few firms who had entered the electronics era earlier. They borrowed heavily to equip themselves with the large design workstations like Lightspeed, Dupont, and Crosfield. These design firms took the first jolts of what heavy capital investment can do to a small company. Some survived, some didn't.

When the Macintosh was developed for graphic design, it wasn't long before great new software was being announced monthly, to enhance the capabilities of these affordable computers. They were slow, but they were cheap when compared to the earlier systems. And that brings in an equation that is still true today. You can have speed or lots of memory or an inexpensive price tag. You can have any two, but not all three. Today, graphic designers use computers and, for the most part, do not use typesetters.

Computers in design will save you time as well as money. When you provide copy on floppy disks, your text can be imported directly into the computer. The Macintosh can take IBM programs such as WordPerfect or Microsoft Word. This means your copy will not be rekeyboarded. It is amazing that in the last thirty years of graphic design, only five or six have been electronic.

You can have speed, lots of memory, or an inexpensive price-tag. You can have any two, but not all three.

Graphic designers are professionals. They care about their profession and they realize, for the most part, they are not fine artists who only create for themselves. Designers can be your best ally. They usually know who are the most dependable service bureaus, color separators, and printers in the area. Many firms will provide management services for those functions and charge an hourly fee. But they prefer that you buy the actual printing, which gives you the advantage of the design firm's expertise, without an additional markup for the printing. A win-win situation for you!

CHAPTER 2

TYPOGRAPHY, PREPRESS, AND PRINTING THEN AND NOW

Typography is an extension of the hand lettering performed by the monks in Europe during the Middle Ages. Type as we know it today began to develop in the fifteenth century, following the invention of movable type. Unless you wish to become a historian, rather than a buyer of graphic arts products and services, you only need to know about the recent history of the industry of typography.

Typography and the Early Years

Let's look at typography in the 1950s. Typesetters were usually a part of a printing plant. Printing was primarily letterpress, meaning that the printing plate came directly in contact with the paper running through the press. There were independent typographers, but they were the exceptions to the rule. As the communications industry started to grow in the 1960s, typographers opened independent trade shops at an accelerated rate.

At this time, typesetting was becoming more specialized, and so was printing. As with other industries, specialization became the response to complexity. We've seen this in medicine and law. No longer are there many general practitioners. There is just too much information to digest. The same has been true of the entire graphic arts industry. With the entrance of total digital technology, the entire printing industry, from graphic design to the waterless presses, has become so complex that specialization has become the rule. Like medicine or law, there are specific areas within the graphic arts that demand special expertise.

Hot Type

Typesetting companies continued to grow both in number and size in the 1970s, with typesetting done by the traditional Linotype machine, which used hot metal to make up lines and blocks of text type. Paper repros were produced from this type on a proofing press. There was an art to pulling repros so that the sheets were consistently perfect.

With the advent of offset printing, printers required camera-ready art. The repro was now ready for the printer to photograph with a copy camera. The repro was photographed and a film negative was created. This negative would later be exposed to a photosensitized aluminum plate. Offset meant that, unlike letterpress, the offset plate passed the ink onto a rubber blanket which then transferred the image to a sheet of paper.

Cold Type

Cold type was the next logical step in the development of typography. Simply put, cold type is the opposite of hot metal. It is a photographic process using photographic paper, which was much more stable than the older repro sheets that used ink. Set photographically, the characters were so sharp that they could be enlarged many times and still look crisp. This was in marked contrast to hot type. The hot type repro, enlarged only slightly, showed the imperfections due to ink on paper.

The only drawback to cold type was the process of setting the type. The typographer would take your marked up manuscript or copy, and keyboard it into the system. This was redundant, since you had already typed the copy once, and also paved the way for errors to occur. In addition, you had to spend more time re-proofreading the re-keyed type. Nevertheless, cold type revolutionized typesetting and the industry thought this would be its biggest revolution.

In the 1980s, cold type became state of the art, combining the typographer's skills with the latest technologies. Typesetting companies grew bigger, and hired more people to satisfy the demands of an information-hungry economy.

The Bullet in the Head of an Industry

Then came desktop publishing. The computer was dismissed by the professional typographers as a poor alternative to typography, which was true at the time. The early programs weren't sophisticated. The typefaces were poor imitations of the type used by the professionals. The spacing etc. was worse than poor. The typographers felt the personal computer was neither a threat nor an ally. Little did they know what was coming. If they had thought about technology in general, they would have realized that anything with this much promise could and would be improved.

Remember the first digital wristwatches? I know someone who paid a thousand dollars for one of the first watches. Now you can get one for under five dollars. This same person also paid a thousand dollars for the first cordless phone, and now everybody has one.

Typographers were slow to realize that their world, as they knew it, was ending. You have to remember, these people were craftsmen, learning their trade through lengthy apprenticeships. They couldn't believe that a machine could make a layperson a typesetter. Maybe they were not typographers, but they were typesetters. This was the end of an industry and a profession.

Type houses have tried to adapt to the new technology by changing into service bureaus. A service bureau takes disks and, through the use of a machine called an imagesetter, generates high-resolution printing negatives or paper positives for printers. This is what is called *output*. Since new equipment had to be purchased, there was an up-front capital expenditure. This seemed the answer, since designers and desktop publishers were not going to buy the expensive imagesetters. There was one wrinkle in the plan. The new service bureaus had lots of customers then. Even printers were using them. This first burst of steam gave these companies a sense of relief. There were still many typographers out of work, but some were being retrained to operate the imagesetters.

The Next Disaster

The evolution wasn't going to stop here. Printers realized that the imagesetting equipment was cheap in contrast to buying the printing presses. They jumped on the bandwagon. Why not generate their own film? And it didn't take them long to realize that they could cut their personnel in the prepress area of their operations. There are still many service bureaus who are just now reacting to this next change. Some have been smart, and let printers buy their operations along with hiring their employees. This was perfect for the printers too, because they would be instantly involved in the technology. No growing pains or slow learning curves. Training would've already taken place, and the bugs would've been worked out of the systems.

There will always be some service bureaus catering to advertising agencies that buy color film for print ads, but there'll only be a handful.

Printing has had Its Own Revolutions

As I mentioned, letterpress was the mainstay of the printing industry in the 1950s. There was gravure printing, but this was used primarily for very long printing runs, and the plates were very expensive. There were both sheet-fed and web letterpresses. Sheet-fed means that single sheets run through a press. Web printing, on the other hand, uses a press that prints on rolls of paper. Sheet-fed is designed for short runs, while while web is best suited for long runs such as magazines and catalogs.

Letterpress was replaced in the 1960s by offset printing. Since a letterpress plate made contact with the sheet, there were drawbacks. The printing images physically flattened the texture of papers. Transitions in color were harsh. The limitations with letterpress were absent in offset printing.

Offset printing, however, uses a plate which never touches the sheet of paper. Instead, a blanket cylinder made of rubber accepts the image from the plate and passes it on to the sheet of paper. Offset uses the principle that oil and water will not mix. The image area on the plate is photographically treated.

With all of the changes in design and production technology, the graphic arts buyer has had to learn new ways of choosing and evaluating suppliers. Let's look at some of these now, beginning with designers.

GRAPHIC DESIGN

Getting the best, but not like the rest.

CHAPTER 3

HOW TO QUALIFY GRAPHIC DESIGNERS

Sounds easy. Just look at their portfolio. Check references. Get them to make a thorough proposal. These are all correct procedures, but there is much more.

No longer is a designer a maker of pretty pictures. They are not artsy-craftsy. This is business and business can be war. As the graphic arts buyer, you are in a very vulnerable position. Even if everyone in your company is on the firing-line daily, you are the one who is exposed the most. You have to produce a printed piece for everyone to look at. The rest of your coworkers can hide behind memos and pointing fingers.

You Are the Client

You have to feel total trust with your design firm. You have to feel *you* are their client, not your company. After all, it is your neck on the line. Many design firms have sales representatives who are savvy in the client/designer relationship. There are also firms that do not have anyone in sales and depend on the principal or principals to perform that function. There is nothing wrong with either one. It's your comfort level that is important.

You may elect to work with "one-person" shops, called

freelancers. With the advent of the computer, there is an even larger cottage industry of these designers. Freelancers are generally cheaper than design firms, because they have less overhead, usually operating out of their homes. You may, on the other hand, elect to work with a full-service design firm.

There are pros and cons to both. You can get lost in a large design firm. You must make it perfectly clear that you want a key contact and an internal back-up. You should also ask for references, including phone numbers, and the kind of work the design firm has produced for them. Discuss their methods of approaching problems, the types of hardware and software they use, and who will be working on your account besides your contacts.

A large design firm has many pluses, too. There is back-up from the other designers in case of illness. The larger firm can usually live past thirty days, if your company's policy is to pay in sixty. (It is best to get this out in the open immediately.) Larger firms can offer different types of talent to suit your project. They tend to attract talented designers because of their stability. There is also a consistency of quality when there is a staff to produce the work. Most large firms will never be too busy to do your work and do it well. The principals of these firms are usually very savvy about print management, photo art direction, and the outsourcing of photography and illustration. Their reputations, if they are good, attract the best printing salespeople, photographers, and illustrators. Larger firms also keep extensive files on all of the current printing papers available, as well as examples of special effects.

Small firms/freelancers are usually less expensive. They will work out of their homes, where the rent for their business is non-existent. Their equipment probably consists of a computer and some software programs. They may do excellent work, but service can be slowed up dramatically in case of the designer's illness, family emergency, or some other personal problem.

Freelancers can be very talented designers who just prefer to work by themselves. It is a good idea to discuss any fears you have with the freelancer, so that contingency plans can be established. Since the one-person shops can only handle one project at a time, you should make sure you don't overload them. You should also try to have your accounts payable department reimburse them promptly, as they often have a tight cash flow situation.

Choosing the Right Designer

Common sense, not just cost, should dictate the type of design firm you use. A good rule of thumb is: the larger the project, the more depth is needed. If you have many small projects and only two or three large ones, it would be wise to have freelancers, as well as the larger firm, involved in the appropriate work. If you are involved in an annual report, a larger firm is probably best. The exception to this is the use of a design consultant. Design consultants can formulate a team of designers to suit the project. They usually operate on a different plane than hands-on freelancers. The drawback is their total availability to you during the project. They can get very busy coordinating everything except you.

Final advice on choosing a designer or design firm is to look at their finished products. Are they successful in reaching the correct audience? Do you feel they will understand your business without an endless learning curve? Do you feel comfortable with them on a social level? This does not mean spending personal time with them, it means they have the social skills to interact with you and others in your company.

A note of warning. There are firms, as well as individuals, who are only selling technology. They may have all of the latest "state-of-the-art" computers. They may produce color separations in-house. But remember, you are buying the design first. In computer design as elsewhere, the bigger the gun doesn't necessarily make the better marksman!

How to Get the Most for Your Design Dollar

As mentioned earlier, graphic design is not fun and games. It's not an unnecessary embellishment of a printed piece, a package, or other visual vehicle. Graphic design has earned an almost religious respect from corporate heavyweights such as IBM, AT&T, MCI, Adidas, Nike, General Motors, Mobil Oil, US Air, etc. They know the power of effective graphics. Why else would an airline place twenty-five foot logos on the tails of their planes? It's not ego. Companies do not throw money around without paybacks. This applies to their design budgets as well.

There is good, mediocre, and bad graphic design. What you get depends on your knowledge and judgement, not your budget. Budgets only restrict how much money you can spend, not how much design you can get. Spend money wisely and you're a corporate hero. But a poor end-product will also be remembered, no matter how much you saved your company in design dollars.

What is good design? It is the effective, attractive, compelling solution to a visual communication problem. How do you achieve this goal? First you start by interviewing graphic designers and categorizing each one of them. It is best to look at both small and large firms. As mentioned earlier, both have advantages. You may wish to use a combination of large and small firms. The larger your company, the greater the probability is that you will need both. There is a lot of different design talent for the different types of projects you will encounter. Let's start with the selection process. This is the foundation for effective design.

The Interview

Before you interview each firm or individual, tell them the type of work your company produces. There is no point in them loading their portfolio full of annual reports if you are primarily producing direct mail pieces.

Budgets only restrict how much money you can spend, not how much design you can get.

During the interview, it is helpful to ask procedural questions. How do they present layouts? How many concepts do they normally show? Do they have an overall hourly rate or do they charge by a project estimate? Even if they charge by the project estimate, they must have an hourly rate for alterations. Is it a flat studio rate or is it different per designer assigned to the project? It is not bad if they have a sliding rate, which simply means that the rate for each designer is a ratio of their salary. Moreover, a more senior designer will work faster, and will charge a higher hourly rate (just as lawyers and accountants have been doing for years).

Overtime is a big consideration. Many firms pay their people straight time for every hour they work. Others pay comp-time, which is time off for overtime hours. Either way, your company pays a single hourly rate, not time-and-a-half or double-time

If you're using IBM equipment for word processing, you should ask what platforms the designer is using for compatibility. The most prevalent programs are: QuarkXPress, Adobe Illustrator and Photoshop, and Aldus Freehand. PageMaker is used by some design firms, but not the majority. QuarkXPress is most popular and, at this time, the most prepress-friendly of any of the page layout software.

If you are interviewing a sales representative or principal of a company, you should ask who will be working on your projects. It is best that you be able to meet with the actual designer. You don't need layers of bureaucracy to get in the way of a time-sensitive project.

Turnaround/scheduling is important. You need to know what normal turnaround is for your kind of work. Most designers and design firms are used to quick turnaround, but this may be reflected in their fees. It's wise to try to keep schedules reasonable, so that when the real crunch comes, the designers know it's not just another false-alarm. I once had a client who said every job was "rush." My reply was, if every job was "rush," then no job was really "rush." Better planning is needed, so that the really critical deadlines will be appreciated by all suppliers involved.

Visit the designers' studios. Once you've come up with a short list of designers, offer to meet in their facilities, if at all possible. This will give you a sense of how they work. Future meetings in the designer's office will save you money, because the designers must bill for travel time if it is during their normal work day.

Getting the Most for the Least

Now that you've selected a designer, designers, or a design studio, it's time to look at how you can get the most for your design dollar. First, prepare for your meeting with the designer. Have a schedule in mind. Know your budget if at all possible. Have rough copy or final copy if it is available. Bring all photos, logos, or other existing artwork that has to be incorporated. Also bring written specifications such as size, approximate number of pages if it is a printed piece, number of colors, key dates, and quantity. Quantity will tell a good designer many things. It will give them parameters such as to whether foil stamping, die cutting, or embossing are practical. Quantity will also have a budget-bearing effect on the the number of colors.

Quantity will often have a bearing on the grade of paper selected. As a rule, small quantities are fine for special effects like stamping or embossing, and the best grades of papers can be used without significant cost increase within your printing budget. Long press runs make special effects expensive, and the grade of paper an overall cost factor. If you're not sure of what is practical, call your printer. Include a rough or final schedule, with key dates.

There are other ways to get more out of your graphic design dollar. You can specify that you want a three-color effect from two colors. This is easy for the pros. You can also achieve classic designs with the use of just black and white. Look at designers' portfolios for this capability. It is an art not every designer can pull off. One color does not have to be black. There are dark PMS colors that look black until they are screened back. Also, there are colored papers that offer a second color look when combined with the right inks.

Tricks of the Trade

What if you have no photographs available and your budget can't afford stock photography or illustration? A good designer can work award-winning wonders with type alone. Believe it or not, charts and graphs can become illustrations. *Fortune* magazine did this in the fifties and sixties. Your project's real restriction isn't money, it's imagination.

Don't be afraid to rough out what you want. A good designer will welcome your organization of the elements. This tells them what you feel is important. It will not restrict them. They will use your sketch as a point of departure. It is

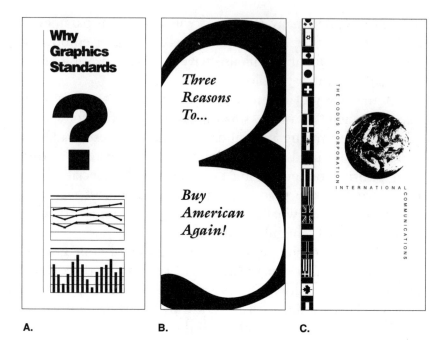

A. *This cover uses generic charts to preview the content of this brochure promoting NIH's Graphics Standards for charts and graphs.*

B. *The number three in the title becomes the graphic cover element for this promotional brochure.*

C. *For the cover of this international public relations firm's brochure, flags were traced and a free black and white photo of the earth from space was obtained from NASA's library.*

very important that you make sure you include all elements that need to be in the final piece. A good designer loves to have things removed. They are never afraid of white space.

It is another thing to add elements after a design is complete. Think of it this way: you design a beautiful living room in your house; each piece of furniture is carefully placed in a spot that maximizes its beauty and functionality. Suddenly someone shows up with a baby grand piano and insists you make room for it. You can't just move some things without destroying the design of the room. The piano is now the dominant element, and the other furniture

The layout below shows how a borrowed photograph and plenty of white space can be dramatic. A good designer can make something out of almost nothing. White space is a friend of the designer and it can be the same for you. The use of an initial cap can also draw the eye of the reader back to the text after the graphic has gotten the first glance.

The
Codus
Corporation

The Codus Corporation

is an international public relations

firm based in Washington D.C.

The firm represents foreign

countries, Fortune five hundred

companies and heads of state.

Codus has been a major player in

the NAFTA Treaty as well as

the new U.S. commerce plan

for Europe.

must work around it. You have to rethink the whole design. The piano is the focal point.

The examples shown on the two previous pages are designs I created with restricted budgets.

The most compelling image on a printed piece is the human figure or face. To prove this, visit a newsstand. When you are standing in front of it, turn your back on the publications. Now, turn around. The publications that feature people on the covers will draw your eye much faster than the ones with cars, motorcycles, or boats. Designers have always known this, and they use it effectively on everything from annual reports to point of sale posters.

The Bid Process

Bidding out graphic design is an effective method of getting the most for your design dollar, but there are dangers. Design is creative, and it is very hard to price creativity. You should write a very tight set of specifications, so each designer or design firm is bidding on the same specifications. This will be covered in the chapter, "How to Write an Effective Bid Request." It is best to conduct a bid conference where all the designers are present and can ask questions in front of one another.

Some companies will allocate a certain amount for several design firms to come up with a design. This is not considered speculation, because the work is being paid for. And you will get a tangible solution to a given problem. There is a danger if the design fee is just a fraction of what the concept time is worth. You can wind up with three really poor designs. At that point, you may as well have paid one firm what you paid all three and gotten a really honest effort. And nine times out of ten, none of the designs would be used and the money has been wasted.

Time is Money

Graphic designers are like accountants or lawyers when it comes to billing. They only have their time to bill for, and time is money. It is also important to realize that most designers care more about their work than the money attached to it. This is important when working with them, because they will give you a lot more in talent and service when they feel their efforts are appreciated.

CHAPTER 4

HOW TO BUY ILLUSTRATION AND PHOTOGRAPHY

There are common-sense rules that apply to the art of buying illustration and photography. Budget is probably the biggest constraint. After all, if you had unlimited funds you could hire LeRoy Nieman or Annie Liebowitz and win all kinds of awards. Unfortunately, in the real world, most of us have to beg, borrow, or steal to get funds for illustration or photography. Somehow, these elements appear, to most bosses, to be the icing on the proverbial cake.

Start a Morgue

Not the kind that holds dead bodies. A morgue is a file or files containing reference materials. In this case, your morgue will contain books on current stock photography, illustrators and reps, special effects, retouchers, and old engravings.

Let's start with illustration. You will probably receive mailings from illustrators or their representatives. If you are new to the field or your company has just created your position for buying graphics, you may need some help in getting started. If you know a graphic designer, they can usually furnish you with illustration sources. If you don't know a designer, look up the local art directors club. Usually those clubs are run by volunteers who are designers. There may be an illustrator's club in your area and this is an even better way to get sources. Also, a local chapter of the American Institute of Graphic Arts (AIGA) can be of assistance. If you're in a remote area, you can contact the national headquarters of the AIGA. Their address is listed in the Appendix.

One of the best ways to work with illustrators is through companies that represent several different artists with different styles. You can discuss budget, concept, and schedule with a representative, who can recommend the best illustrator for your project. Sometimes this can be a big plus, because you don't have to bring these delicate topics into your conversation with the artist you have chosen to work with.

Don't be afraid of logistics. I've worked with illustrators on the other side of the country. With fax machines, you can receive rough layouts as quickly as if your artist was in the same city. In fact, often quicker than I used to receive them before fax machines. Once you have approved a sketch, the final illustration can be sent to you overnight.

Low Budget, Big Results

Let's say you have a brochure with no budget for illustrations, and there are no photographs available. How can you make the brochure visually compelling?

First, are there charts in the text? A good designer can design a chart to be an illustration. If there are no charts, a good designer can make the typography exciting. What if you have several really mediocre photos that have been overused? A good designer can *convert* the photos to *line conversions* that will look dynamic and exciting. The key is to use a good designer (see pages 30 and 31). I've even used a photo copier to make high-contrast images.

Location Photography

Location photography is an art. It's best to have reviewed as many portfolios as possible. They'll beat down your door, once they know you are a buyer. But, if you're in a remote area, get a copy of the *Corporate Showcase*. This publication, and the others listed in the Appendix, will give you mini-portfolios on photographers as well as on illustrators and designers all over the country. If you're in a large metropolitan area, there may be local source books available.

For a listing of professional photographers, contact the American Society of Media Photographers (ASMP) in your area. If there is no local ASMP, the national headquarter's address is also listed in the Appendix.

How is Location Photography Bought?

The majority of location photographers charge by the day. This is called their day-rate, and usually doesn't include any expenses. All you get is the person behind the camera. Their assistant, travel, food, lodging, film, and processing is all extra. It's best to get an estimate of what the photographer feels will be incurred. Also, photographers limit the usage of their photos. You must negotiate if you want unlimited usage. Your photos may also be sold as stock by the photographer, after you use them, unless you have made an agreement to the contrary. The photographer's estimate should spell out these conditions, but again, your purchase order can contradict them. If the photo subjects include people, make sure the photographer gets signed *releases* from everyone in the photographs.

Location photographers can also charge by the photograph. If this is the case, there are probably still expenses not included in the fee. Here again, get an estimate of the expenses and a usage agreement. Remember, everything is negotiable. Don't let anyone dictate terms you feel are unfair.

But remember, everything must be agreed upon, in writing, before the assignment starts, not after.

If the location photography is part of a graphic design project and a layout has been produced, the designer should, if at all possible, art direct the photography on location. This will ensure that the graphic feeling within the layout is maintained. The same estimate principles apply to the graphic designer. Get costs from them for art direction as well as contemplated expenses.

There are several good books on this subject. Allworth Press' *Pricing Photography* and the Graphic Artists Guild's *P.E.G.s* are two excellent sources for this information.

Is Studio Photography Different from Location?

Studio photography is similar to location. The same principles apply to estimates. You should always be welcome at any photo shoot, location or studio. This is insurance for the photographer. Studio photography is usually billed by the image. With assignments such as catalogs, either a day-rate or a cost per picture can be used. You must also discuss your use of the photos with the photographer. Their usage fees vary. If you want unlimited use, you will usually pay a premium. This is also called a *buy-out*.

Stock Photography: the Good and the Bad

The good part of using stock photography is that there are no hidden expenses from the photographer. The fee charged for the stock photos is usually negotiable, and will vary by the type of publication, number of copies printed, whether the photo is on the cover, the size of the photo etc.

The downside is that your photo may have been used before by someone else. Also, it's difficult to find exactly what you want in a stock photo, which can cost you anywhere from a couple of hundred dollars to a thousand or more. Most stock photos will cost you a minimum of fifteen hundred dollars if lost. This is because you have the original, not a duplicate. If a stock-house sends you thirty slides to review and something happens to them, you're out forty-five thousand dollars. Make sure your insurance covers this exposure.

The Bettman Archive offers a source book of old photographs, engravings and reproductions of paintings. These images are sold in the same way as other stock photographs.

CHAPTER 5

HOW TO PROOFREAD
LIKE A PRO

Proofreading is a necessity in business. No matter what your position in a company, if you have to review anything written, you need to know how to mark up a proof. You may be the president of your company, but you still have to communicate. Use of the correct proofreading marks communicates in a universal language, leaving nothing to chance.

To understand proofreading you must know the fundamentals of type. Type is set in point sizes. Each typeface has the various assortments of special characters to enable the face to handle most any situation. Any one size and style of type is considered a font. Lower case letters are the small characters, and upper case are the capital letters. The typographers of old used to keep the letters in two cases. The top one held the capital letters, thus called upper case, and the bottom held what we call the lower case.

There are two basic type styles. They are serif and sans serif. Sans serif means without serifs, which are little "feet" at the tops and bottoms of letters. This book is set in serif type.

There is an ongoing battle over the readability of sans serif versus serif. I was told once, by a righteous editor, that I should not use sans-serif type because it was not readable. I was also told that I should never reverse type out of a color *(reverse* is the use of white type on a black or color background). I asked this editor if the U.S. Department of Transportation had a death wish for the American public, because most of our signs on the nation's interstates have reversed sans-serif letters.

ABC is a serif type style.

ABC is a sans serif type style.

On the following pages we will look at the basics of proofreading copy and effectively marking the corrections. Don't be afraid of writing a note if you feel the proofreading marks are too cryptic. After all, we are not trying to show off our new skills, we're trying to communicate. This same rule holds true in marking up a printer's proof. You should be as straightforward as possible.

If you don't know certain printing terms, don't try to fake it. Use everyday English in explaining what you want to see. Also, don't be afraid to draw a sketch or diagram of what you want. The printer doesn't want to guess any more than you want them to.

Photocopy the page with the proofreading marks. Keep it where your proofing is generally done. Going over the corrections with the printer or designer in person is the optimum way to communicate, because they can ask questions immediately. In this day of voice mail and "telephone tag," nothing outweighs a person-to-person meeting.

If you are a writer or an editor, you can probably skip the following pages. Even so, you might learn something new. In reviewing the marks, I found several that I had been using incorrectly. This is no time to stop being a professional.

Proofreading Marks

Caps All caps

ˇ Apostrophe-'single quote'

bf Bold face

✗ Broken type

ˇ Close quotes

⌒ Close up space

⊙ Colon

∧ Comma

/–/ Dash

ℓ Delete/close up

ℓ Delete/remove⟋ℓ

□ Em space/indent

⟨⋯⟩ Ellipsis

!/ Exclamation point

⌐ Flush left

⌐ Flush right

⹀ Horizontally align

= Hyphen

stet Ignore marks

caps Initial caps

Insert space

ital Italicize

ℓ/ʂ Letter space

lf Light face

lc Lower CASE

⊔ Lower words or letters

flush¶ No indent

ok w/c Okay with corrections

ˇ Open quotes

¶ Paragraph

(/) Parenthesis

⊙ Period

?/ Question mark

⊓ Raise words or letters

rom *Roman* type

no ¶ Run in

ⓙ Semi colon

sc Small caps

⟨*sp*⟩ Spell out

tr Transpose letters

‖ Vertically align

wf Wrong Font

Proofing Copy

Example:

cap these paragraphs have ben set to give you an *tr*

example of how proof reading marks work. Note

that both sides of the (copy) block is used for the *ff*

marks.

no¶ It is important, to know ho to use *these* marks *w*

correctly, because they're universal in communicat-

ing instructions.

wf Now that everyone can typeset on a computer, it #

is more important than ever, to the use correct *tr*

proofreeding symbols. Practice corecting copy you *r*

lc RECIEVE without looking at the examples to see

how much you've retained.

This copy does not contain all of the marks we

cap have covered. i have used the ones most common

to give you a feel for what a "marked up" page =

would look like The methods for using the rest of

the marks should be apparent from what has been *l*

marked here.

Proofed Copy

Example:

These paragraphs have been set to give you an example of how proofreading marks work. Note that both sides of the copy block is used for the marks. It is important, to know ho to use these marks correctly, because they're universal in communicating instructions.

Now that everyone can typeset on a computer, it is more important than ever, to the use correct proofreading symbols. Practice correcting copy you recieve without looking at the examples to see how much you've retained.

This copy does not contain all of the marks we have covered. I have used the ones most common to give you a feel for what a marked-up page would look like. The methods for using the rest of the marks should be apparent from what has been marked here.

When marking proofs, you should always use a different color than the color of the text. If the text is black, a red pen is best. This will highlight your marks, leaving less chance of missed corrections. It's a good idea to have several different types of pens and markers handy. I keep a glass of them next to my desk. Also, proofs come with different surfaces and textures. For example, a blueline is on photographic paper and a marker works better than a ballpoint pen. 3M col-orkeys are on mylar, and a china marker works best on this surface.

Remember, only you can control your own alteration charges.

With the new technology, page proofs are usually generated first, skipping the galley stage completely. The advantage to this is you get to see how the type works with the graphics and photographs. You can rewrite a sentence if you don't care for the way it breaks. If you are thorough, you can minimize your alteration charges by using this proof to work out all of your format problems. If you're careless and just mark typesetting corrections, you may later have to re-mark the proof to accommodate the layout changes caused by your editing.

Alteration Charges/Change Orders

Remember, only you can control your own alteration charges. If you work for a large company and there many people who have to approve the proofs, here are some helpful tips. Give anyone other than the last person who has to sign-off only one shot at correcting their section of the copy. Get the copy to the last person as soon as possible, and make sure that major changes are made *early* in the proofing process. Try to have as few people proof the blueline as possible.

The more important the project is, the more true this becomes. I designed an annual report for a major corporation. When the blueline was presented to the president, he was on his way to Europe for an emergency meeting. He took the blueline on the airplane with him, and for seven hours he scrutinized every word in it. When I got it back, the entire annual report had to be reset and re-laid out. This was not only time consuming, but very expensive. If you are ever working on an annual report for your company, remember that this is the president's message to the stockholders. All of the corporate palace guard's opinions mean nothing if the president doesn't agree.

CHAPTER 6

HOW THE NEW ELECTRONIC DESIGN TECHNOLOGY CAN HELP YOU

This chapter is not meant to intimidate you, so I'll stick to the basics. *The computer age is here and everyone is in it for good.* There's no turning back. At this writing, there are designers who refuse to use a computer. They believe the computer has killed good design. I beg to differ with them. Bad designers have hurt electronic design.

In many cases, the problems of the new technology are those of perception. I was interviewed by phone on how the computer has affected my business. Most of the questions were leading, and told me exactly what the interviewer thought. For example, I was asked: Were clients making more changes because the computer would allow them to? Was the capital investment in new equipment hurting my cash flow? Had the quality of design declined because of the electronics? Did I feel the printing industry was receiving inferior electronic files from designers? I could only answer from my own perspective, and the answer was "no" on all counts. It seemed the interviewer had already made up her mind, and even now, I don't know if I changed her mind.

It reminded me a bit of the story of the blind men and the elephant. Each of the blind men described his perception of the elephant by the part he was touching. One of the men, touching the elephant's leg, said "The elephant is like a tree." Another man held the elephant's tail and exclaimed, "No, an elephant is like a snake." Each man was partially correct from his own vantage point, but their knowledge of the whole picture would be forever lacking. This is human nature. We only believe what we perceive.

I have spoken to printers who have cursed computers, designers with computers, and software programs that wouldn't allow correct trapping (the fit of colors butting each other). These same printers, six months later, told me, candidly, that they were now immersed in the new technology, and would never go back to the conventional methods of stripping even if they could. I asked them to sum up the advantages. The answers were, "Computerized prepress is faster and more accurate, it takes less labor, and the capital investment is peanuts when compared to the cost of new presses and other equipment."

How to Save Real Money

The new technology can, in fact, be your greatest ally. You can show true cost as well as time savings. Once again, remember that all services that someone else buys for you are going to be marked up. Even if they tell you otherwise, you're going to pay somewhere. No one can stay in business giving away services, and brokering is a service.

With this in mind, find a good service bureau. Usually a former typographer, the bureau can supply you with high resolution paper or film output. On the other hand, if you place ads, you can buy your own negatives. If you're in charge of a publication, you can furnish your printer with film. Make sure you get a printing quote with and without film, so you can compare costs.

You can also save by using one of the many printers who are now entering the electronic prepress arena, with in-house service. However, it makes more sense for you to buy your own film if your printer does not have an in-house capability of generating negatives electronically.

Some printers will tell you they have the ability to take your electronic files. This does not mean they are not farming out their prepress services. Ask them point-blank if they are. Don't be timid. It's a justifiable concern and deserves a direct response.

If your company hasn't made the shift to using disks for copy, do it now. Most design and printing companies are working with IBM WordPerfect or Microsoft Word disks. Don't use double-density disks, which are only good on IBM compatible systems. Go through your company and confiscate them, then make sure everyone has a supply of high-density disks.

The Macintosh will easily convert IBM programs into files that can be imported into QuarkXPress and PageMaker. If you are looking into page-layout software, get QuarkXPress. In my opinion, it is the better of the two basic page-layout systems. It's more expensive but also much more printer and designer friendly.

How to Find Free Consultants

Your biggest allies are your vendors. Use them as consultants and call them if there is a procedure you're not sure of. Remember, they won't laugh at a question and they're not in a position to use your lack of knowledge to make you look bad in your company. There are some people who, when lost in a new city, will never ask for directions. Just think, if their time was worth money, how stupid this would be. And your time is worth money.

I have watched savvy designers guess about the answers to questions a printer could have answered instantly. This may be human nature, but it doesn't have to be yours. And you will look good when you seem to have solved a technical problem all by yourself.

Beware of Computer Gurus

There are designers and professional consultants who are ready, at a moment's notice, to tell you about their insights into electronic design and prepress technology. Beware. I have heard some really "off the wall" observations from these so-called consultants. These people can be like the blind men and the elephant. They only see what they have been exposed to, and have a closed mind to other areas. A good example of this is the salesman of computer hardware and software, who will try to make you believe that their product is the best. They often convince the so-called guru, and now it's gospel.

You need to get answers, because money is at stake. Call some experienced peers. These people, like you, depend on the right answers. We will get into networking later in this book, but right now, meet others whose responsibilities in their companies are similar to yours. You probably get two or three invitations a week to trade shows, lectures, industry seminars, and conferences. Take advantage of them.

The Electronic Design and Prepress Process

You can skip this section if you're already prepress literate. Then again, you may learn one thing you didn't know and this little bit of reading will have been worth the effort.

To understand what's happening today, one must understand how things were done before the computer.

Let's start with the conventional design process. The designer would meet with you and discuss the project. They would go over the budget, copy, and schedule. The designer would develop thumbnail layouts to form a direction. These are miniatures of pages, sometimes in color, sometimes not.

Most likely, these sketches would not be shown to you.

The designer would order layout type from a local type-setter, paste it on a board, and make a photostat or send out for an INT. An INT is an instant transfer and can be bur-nished onto almost any paper surface, much like press-type, but they were expensive, because film negatives had to be made first. Once the INT was in position, the designer would add screens and solid blocks of color with Zip-A-Tone colored film. If there were color photographs, the designer would send the original to a photo lab and have prints made. These prints would then be cropped, cut, and pasted into the layout, which was called a comprehensive.

If the project was a multi-page brochure, a cover and several facing page spreads would be produced as compre-hensives. Once you approved these layouts, the designer would order rough galleys of running text. Your manuscript would be keyboarded again by the typographer. In the sev-enties, linotype proofs were pulled on uncoated paper for proofing and for the designer to paste into the rest of the layout. The galleys were also referred to as readers. Made from hot type, these galleys were relatively slow and cum-bersome to produce.

A Revolution?

Remember what happened in the late seventies? Cold-type made its debut, with characters formed through a photo-graphic process and reproduced on RC paper. The type was much cleaner and was so sharp that it could be enlarged and still look good, which was not true with hot-type. If a word was enlarged photographically, the imperfections or feather-ing would show. The cold-type reading galleys were photo-copies, and much more durable than the lino proofs. Designers thought they were watching a revolution of bibli-cal proportions. Little did they know what was coming.

In a related development, waxers (machines that would use hot wax) replaced the messy glue pots of rubber cement. Still, the designer would paste the running galleys into what was called a tackdown. This was a dummy, and it would show you how all of the pages laid out. A laborious task, but it had to be done.

Once the tackdown was approved, the designer would paste up the final repros, and you would once more check those boards. The final boards were also called the final art or mechanicals. These were sent to the printer, where they would be photographed. Negatives would be produced and exposed to a special paper. This was the blueline proof. Once you approved the blueline, the negatives would be used to create photosensitized printing plates. The next step was the actual printing process.

Let's look at the real revolution. With the advent of the computer, the face of graphic design and prepress changed forever.

The same design project would still start with you and the designer meeting. You would still discuss budget, copy, and schedule. This time, however, your copy is on a floppy disk.

Some The Same, A Lot New

The designer would begin with thumbnails just as before, but then the design process would change dramatically. The disk would be inserted into the designer's computer and converted to a Macintosh file. Your disk would remain IBM, but on the designer's hard drive, it would become text that could be formatted into a layout. The layouts for a cover and sample spreads would be created. Photos in color, or black and white, would be scanned into the layout. Tint blocks of color would be created. Color laser proofs would be produced on the actual paper. No outside costs would be incurred from typesetters or photo labs and then passed on to you. Not to mention the savings in time.

With the initial layout approved, the designer would continue to work with the copy from your original disk. There would be no rekeyboarding of your text, thus greatly reducing the chances for PEs. These are *printer's errors* or mistakes made by the person setting you type.

The designer would now produce proofs of each complete page on a 300 or 600 DPI laser printer, so that what you proof is the same as the final mechanical, only lower resolution. This takes the place of an interim tackdown. You skip the galley stage completely, and get to look at page proofs first.

You are in an electronic revolution, and reaping the benefits of the new computer technology.

If you never went through the old proofing stages, you can't really appreciate the speed that is gained, not to mention the fact that you are proofing a live page. This saves days, not to mention dollars. You are in an electronic revolution, and reaping the benefits of the new computer technology. With all these changes, design costs have dropped, and it's your gain. Let's compare the costs of the old and the new approaches to a typical design project. In this case, it's a corporate capabilities brochure.

We'll look not only at costs, but at the stages necessary in completing the project. Naturally the more stages, thus more labor, the more the job will cost. You can also save money by pre-proofing your copy prior to giving it to a designer. If you're using a data processing program and you will furnish the designer with a disk, strip out all of your hard returns, bullets, indents, etc. But, you should give the designer your hard-copy with these commands in it.

Specifications: *Design and production of an 8.5" x 11", 16 page/self-cover, 4-color brochure, with 24 color subjects averaging 7" x 10", Stock is 80# Lustro Offset Enamel Cover.*

1. Conventional/Pre-Computers

Layout of Cover and Two Spreads (labor)	$1,250.00
Layout Typography	125.00
Six Instant Dry Transfers @ $65.00 each	390.00
Six C-Prints/with Internegs @ $45.00 each set	270.00
Typography for Entire 16 Pages	800.00
Tackdown of 16 Pages	800.00
Paste-up of 16 Pages	800.00
Total	**$4,435.00**

2.Computerized Layout and Design Production

Layout of Cover and Two Spreads (labor)	$1,250.00
Color Output for Comprehensives	600.00
Design Production of 16 Pages	800.00
Syquest Disk and 300 DPI Proofs	150.00
Total	**$2,800.00**

As you can see, the electronic design process has saved $1,635.00, or nearly thirty-seven percent, as well as many hours of time. These are real dollars and real savings.

Once you approve the page proofs, the designer's disk is given to the printer. If you decide to buy your own film, you simply send the disk to your service bureau and request them to send your negatives to your printer. If the disk goes to the printer because they have in-house capabilities, the printer will generate film directly from the designer's disk.

Next, a blueline is pulled just like before. From here on, the printing process is similar to the way it always has been. Yes, there are waterless presses and computerized consoles on the printing presses. There are five, six, seven, and eight color presses, but it's still ink on paper. There is a revolution coming in printing, but I'll get into that later.

CHAPTER 7

HOW TO WRITE AN EFFECTIVE DESIGN BID REQUEST

T he most important factor in the success of a design project is the bid process. The expression "apples and oranges" is quite appropriate. It is very important that if several designers are bidding on a project, they each bid on the same requirements or specifications. Good written information is an absolute necessity, and a meeting with all parties at the same time is the optimum. Many companies simply send out a Request For Proposal (RFP). Another name for this is a Request For Quotation (RFQ). The U.S. Government has a better system. They hold formal bid conferences and they bid out everything.

The Bid Conference

You are actually doing yourself a disservice by not holding a formal bid conference. When all of the designers are present at once, they can ask questions and each of them will hear the answers. If one designer receives an RFP in the mail or in an individual meeting, that designer may have a legitimate question or, even better, a more economical suggestion for producing the job. If the idea has genuine merit and changes the scope of work, you must notify the other designers, individually, of the new specifications. The bid conference, on the other hand, can be a hotbed of good ideas, if you let the participants feel they are shaping the project for the better.

There is another "Apple and Orange" factor to be considered. The design firms for the project should be approximately the same type and size, except for small projects that usually don't warrant a full-fledged bid conference, the types of firms or individual designers should be of equal talent and capability. If you elect to use either freelancers (one-person companies) or large design firms, it is better that they are similar to each other. You wouldn't invite a large printer and a quick-print shop to the same bid conference for a printing project. The same holds true with design firms.

Be Thorough

The greatest mistake in writing specifications is not being clear about what you expect. Use a businesslike tone if you like, but don't forget common sense. For instance, I recently received a RFP for a complex project. The client was very explicit about the quality expected, the deadline, the number of colors, and the dimensions. But the number of pages was missing. When I asked about the page count, I was told there would be between twenty and thirty. My client was very busy and didn't want to get into a discussion about the project.

Since the specs told me the project was a saddle stitched brochure, I knew the number of pages had to be divisible by four. (Four pages equal one sheet bound in a saddle stitched brochure, as you can see if you pull the staples out of a *Time* magazine.) Also, the most economical way to run this job is in multiples of eights or sixteens. Neither was an option without a discussion with the client. So, to solve the dilemma and make sure I would be covered, I simply gave a per-page price. I don't know what my competition did. I do know the client was going to be even busier later, trying to get comparative bids.

An RFP can be as simple or as complex as you want it to be. Let's look at the most complex because, after that, you can decide what you want to omit. There are usually three parts to a bid requested in a RFP. The first is the design firm's *capabilities statement*. The second is their *technical proposal* or *project overview*. The third is the *cost proposal*. Each of the three is said to carry equal weight. Cost is a consideration when each firm has met the other criteria.

I have also seen some companies ask for a layout with the proposal. This is against the American Institute of Graphic Arts and the Graphic Artists Guild's Codes of Ethics, and it is also against the International Design by Electronics Association's Trade Customs, if the designer subscribes to any of these (the Graphic Design Trade Customs are reviewed in this book). This issue is currently under review due to FTC issues. It has been determined by the United States Justice Department that no one can stop a designer from doing spec work as this, they feel, causes the restriction of competition. But I feel the majority of designers in the industry believe that it is unethical to ask for such services.

After a thorough portfolio review with each participating design firm, and the submission of a detailed proposal, you should have enough input to make an intelligent decision. Design firms, unlike advertising agencies, are not counting on millions of dollars in ad revenues to enable them offer free or speculative work. They bill by the hour for services rendered. (Spec work is free work, and it's usually worth what you pay for it.)

Some companies, who wish to see multiple concepts, will offer each firm an equal fee to come up with a design concept. If the fee is just a token, you may get three inferior designs and thus an inferior final product.

The Request for Proposal (RFP)

The Letter: A letter introducing the project is the usual way to invite the design firms to bid on a project. Even with a person-to-person bid conference, a letter is a proper enclosure with the project specifications. The letter should give an overview of the project from your standpoint. Be sure to describe the level of quality expected. Your review process and any other pertinent information, including the due date for the proposal and the award date, should be included. You should also include your name and telephone number, if you are the key contact in your company who can answer questions. If you are not the person who can answer questions, include that person's number. The letter should reference each part of the RFP, which is helpful if something is inadvertently left out.

Remember, it's to your advantage to make the RFP as clear as possible. You don't need phone calls from the bidders because of unclear specifications. They may think you don't know your job, and this sign of weakness could come back to haunt you later.

1. Statement of Work and Requirements: This part of the RFP contains several key elements that explain to the bidder the scope of work, as well as what you will provide.

A. Background. This is the history of the project, if it has one, and the purpose of the piece to be designed. Also, you can describe the company's history and goals/purpose. This overview is important in the understanding of how your company does business.

B. Work Requirement. A complete description of the project's specifications, such as: size, number of pages, number of colors, photographic or illustration treatments, methods of presentation of layouts and page proofs, how your copy is prepared (on disk or not), and number of copies to be printed. This is the "Meat and Potatoes" of the project. Any special requirements should be highlighted in this section.

C. Project Management. This is the request for a technical proposal. The technical proposal is a description of the scope of work from the designer's point of view, as well as their insights as to how the project's process can be improved. This is not a request for verbal descriptions of design solutions, nor for free design consultation. It is meant to show you that the designer isn't going to approach your project with a cookie-cutter or standardized method. You are paying for a custom job, and you should accept no less.

2. Evaluation Criteria: This is an explanation of how each proposal will be judged. You can assign importance to each facet of the proposal, which will usually be evaluated in accordance with the following factors:

A. Project Staff Profiles. The biographies of the staff who will be assigned to this project.

B. Time-line Management. The specific time-line for completing the project.

C. Capability and Experience. A description of the design firms experience working with companies similar to yours as well as projects similar to the one in the RFP.

D. General Approach. These are the plans or procedures for ensuring: timeliness, cost effectiveness, and the high quality of the finished product.

E. Work Statement/Technical Proposal. A complete description by the designer, of the work to be performed and the methods to be used. The designer may be invited to critique the previous project, if there was one.

Unlike the general approach, this is meant to show you that the designer understands your specific requirements. If you have any unusual requirements, or specific procedures that the designer has to comply with, they should be noted in the RFP.

F. Cost Proposal. The cost proposal should contain only the cost of work and expenses spelled out in your *Statement of Work and Requirements.* Author's alterations, unless you know exactly what they will be and can convey this to the designer, should not be expected to be included in the quote. Other unknown out-of-pocket expenses must also be excluded. Hourly rates can be assigned by the designers for services that may be needed, such as print management, photo art direction, illustration, preparation of charts and graphs, copy preparation, keyboarding of text, and anything else that may be part of the scope of work, but have not yet been defined. Most companies use cost as a parameter, not as a specific criteria, in evaluating the proposal.

The Bids Are In, But There's a Problem

One of the quotes is twice as high as the next one and the lowest is too low to be realistic. It's safe to say that your RFP wasn't clear. That is not to say you weren't detailed enough, only that some element or elements were interpreted differently in the bidders' minds. The first thing to do is examine each *technical proposal,* to see if the designers understood the scope of the work.

If the proposals seem to be in order, you may wish to rebid the project with several other designers. The obvious quick solution, however, if time is against you, is to award the job to the middle bidder.

PREPRESS & PRINTING

They're an art, as much as art itself.

CHAPTER 8

HOW TO SELECT
A PRINTER

This sounds simple. So why devote a chapter to it? All you do is get out the phone book and look up a printer. There are probably plenty of them, if you are in a metropolitan area. In a small town you have fewer to choose from locally, but in the age of the fax machine, computer modems, and overnight delivery services, out of town printers are easily accessible.

Printers are as different as people, because they are people. But printing plants usually operate in similar ways, because their managers have come from other printing plants, bringing with them some bad habits as well as some valuable improvements.

The Types of Printers You Will Need

There are three or four types of printers that can serve your basic needs. If your company doesn't have an in-house printing division, you need a small quick-print shop for simple one color jobs. Look for a commercial printer who recognizes that business printing is always time-driven, instead of a large chain, which usually caters to casual, walk-in customers. Word of mouth referrals are the best. If you can find another company similar to yours in size and in your general area, their print buyer has probably found a good source, and will be happy to share it with you. (That is, unless you're a competitor.)

Because of the nature of quick-print projects, you probably won't have to bid this work out. I suggest that, in the beginning, you get several competitive quotes for a typical project. Then every six months, bid out a project, just to keep the printer from thinking you're in his own private shooting gallery.

One and Two-Color Sheetfed

Once you have a quick-print source, you probably need a printer who specializes in two-color work. In this age of tight budgets, most corporate and association printing is one or two colors. This same company may be able to handle your four-color needs as well, if it has a mix of two- and four-color presses.

> *You should not only interview printing salespeople, you should also meet their Customer Service Representative (CSR).*

Finding this printer or group of printers to bid on projects is best done through the referral process. You should not only interview the printing salespeople, but also meet their Customer Service Representative (CSR). This is the person with whom you're going to spend the most time. The printing salespeople are constantly out making calls, so you need access to their in-house personal assistant.

The most frustrating thing a printing company can have, in my opinion, is *voice mail.* Service organizations that have voice mail, have abusers. When your project is on dead-line, you call the CSR because you urgently need an answer to a critical question. If they have voice mail, they will call you back, but by then you may be in a meeting with your boss and can't take the call. I have dialed zero for the opera-tor to page the CSR, and then have gotten her voice mail. There is no substitute for human contact.

Four-Color Sheetfed

If your company produces high-end four or more color pub-lications, you will need a printer who specializes in this kind of work. Here again, the referral method is best. This type of printer may be able to handle your two-color needs as well. But be careful, because the reverse is not always true. Some two-color printers will say they can handle your four-color projects on a two-color press, but this is neither cost effective or smart.

It's impossible to effectively press inspect a four-color job when two colors are printed at different times. The first pass is dry, and the second pass is the only one that can be controlled by the pressman. If there's a problem with the ink densities of the first pass, it's too late for a correction. With a four-color press, however, the pressman can adjust any of the colors at any time, which is especially crucial when flesh tones are involved.

Web Printers

With a publication, catalog, or annual report that is printed in large quantities, you will probably need a printer who has a web press, which prints off rolls of paper. These presses are very fast, and they print on both sides of the sheet at the same time. A word of warning, though: It's best that the printer you choose have a backup press. Web presses are complicated machines, and can break down. If this happens, and your job is on a tight deadline, you need to make sure the printer can run your job on another press. There are large and small web presses. Find out from a neutral source, such as your designer, which size web press is best suited for your publication.

In interviewing printers, I suggest you take a tour of the plant. This is not just for PR, but to let you note several important things, such as: How busy are they? Who are their customers? How advanced is their prepress area? Do they have proper facilities for press checks (meaning an area other than the press room with a light box for viewing proofs)? A printing plant's personality will show when you see it in action.

Press Inspections

Important projects often demand press inspections. Get yourself a printer's loupe, which is a magnifying glass that printers use to check registration and screen densities. You should also bring any previous proofs with you, if the printer doesn't already have them there.

Press inspections are very important. They are sometimes referred to as "on-sites." There is a psychological factor at work when a printer knows you are coming to check your job, and printers may even boast about catching problems before you arrive. When a job will have a press inspection, it automatically gains an added sense of importance.

There are some important rules to follow when you perform a press inspection. First, make sure all blueline corrections were made; it can be disastrous if you just assume that they were. Second, make sure you have all original color transparencies, artwork, layouts etc. with you when you are checking the press sheets. Third, look at color subjects upside down as well as right side up, so that the picture itself will not distract your eye from being objective. Check the registration. If there is a fifth or sixth PMS ink (color), make sure you have your own swatch and check the match on the sheet. The printer may have a PMS book that is old and the colors may not be as true as your own book.

Fourth, if there are solid areas of color, ask the printer for a densitometer reading. This instrument, which looks like a big desk stapler, allows the pressman to check the amount of ink on the sheet. Last but not least, okay a sheet for the pressman, date it and sign it. Now, and most important, do the same thing for yourself, because your copy can be crucial. I once had a designer come back from a press inspection without a duplicate of the okayed press sheet. Sure enough, the job was bad. We asked the printer if we could see the okayed press sheet. We were told it was lost, but it had been the same as the unacceptable final piece. We didn't have a leg to stand on. Don't let this happen to you!

CHAPTER 9

HOW TO SELECT PRINTING PAPERS

Appropriate choice of paper is the second most important part of a printed piece. Design is probably first, because a good design on the cheapest paper can still be effective. Knowing what papers are best suited for what types of printing projects is the only way to specify the best sheet for the job. There are many choices, but a knowledge of paper will narrow those choices down. For example, if a particular paper is very expensive but your print run is small (less than 5,000 copies), the price of paper is not much of an overall cost factor in the printing price. On the other hand, if you're printing a large quantity (anything over 5,000 copies) paper can be a significant cost factor. Thus, within your particular budget, the paper's part of the total printing cost, is a sliding one.

The "No-Brainer"

Selecting the right paper is an art form. You can limp along using the same papers over and over. No one will question you if your standby sheet is a good sheet. But many people, including good designers, use the same papers over and over again, from laziness or lack of knowledge. Also, the computer has made it easier to show designs on white paper (the color-output printers require white paper), thus many designers are not using the exciting colors and textures available.

The Paper Merchant

Paper merchants are wholesalers, and they can help you learn more about paper, if you know how to use them. They stock a certain amount of the popular papers. If a particular type of paper is not on their floor, they can usually get it overnight from the paper mill.

The relationship between the merchant and the mill has undergone some interesting changes over the years. Each merchant used to have exclusive rights to sell a certain mill's papers, so that the competition was more between mills than merchants. The mills promoted their own papers through advertising and through mill trips, which enabled them to wine and dine printers and designers. In the seventies, however, the mills got smart and decided to make the merchants scramble. They gave more than one merchant in an area the right to sell their papers. Now each merchant usually represents several different mills. To show you their stock, merchants make up shoebox-type boxes containing all of their samples, and you can get one from your local paper merchants' sales-promotion person. They will call on you and bring a fresh box, which is important because certain papers are discontinued, while others add new grades or change colors. This same representative will come in from time to time and upgrade the box. But remember, out of sight, out of mind. If you don't call them every six months or so, they may forget to perform this service.

There are charts that compare grades and costs of competing sheets and these are also available from the local merchants in your area, or the mills themselves.

Paper Production and What You Need to Know

Paper is manufactured primarily from wood pulp. The wood is stripped of bark, ground up, and turned into usable pulp by means of heat, chemicals, or mechanical grinding. Once the pulp is in a semi-liquid form, it is bleached. This gives the finished papers their brightness. Less bleaching leaves the paper browner, as in grocery bags. After bleaching, dyes and fillers are added to give the sheet a specific color, and various properties are incorporated, such as rag content from cotton fibers, or titanium oxide for opacity and brightness.

The modern papermaking machines are very complex, usually made up of three sections. First, the pulp is fed into the wet end. Then, it is forced into the second area, called the press section. Here, the water is pressed out between rolls and felts. A dandy roll is used to compress the sheet and distribute the fibers. The dandy roll may carry a design on it to give the paper a watermark. The third section, is where the product is dried to the desired level in a machine composed on steam-heated, cast-iron drums. Now it has changed from a watery mush to paper that is recognizable as such. After this process, the paper is calendered or finished. Coatings are added if the paper is to become a coated sheet.

Paper Characteristics

The Sheet: Paper has two sides. There is a wire side, which is the side of the sheet exposed to the wire in the press section. The other side is the felt side or top side, which was exposed to the dandy roll. This is the smoothest side of the sheet.

Paper Finish: This is the texture or smoothness of a sheet of paper. The usual finishes (by rough to smooth) are antique, eggshell, vellum, machine finished and coated. Finishes can also be embossed into the paper through the use of rotary embossing machines. Tweed, linen, and ribbed textures are just some of the patterns used.

I recently used a sheet named Champion Benefit Vertical Cover. The swatch book showed the sheet with grooves running up and down, so I assumed the the paper was made that way. Most grooved or ribbed sheets come with the the lines running horizontally.

I asked three printers for quotes on my printing specs. I received the prices and released the artwork (disk) to the low bidder. When the printer realized the grooves were designed to run vertically, I was notified that there would be an extra cost of $225 because the grooves ran horizontally and this would cause excessive waste. The printer said that he could not get as many covers out of a press sheet as he had estimated and more paper would be needed.

I was not happy. It had been my responsibility to get the quotes, and I didn't feel I could call my client and ask for more money. I contacted the merchant and lodged a complaint. If the sheet had not been named Vertical Cover, I would've checked on the direction of the grooves. I am still waiting to hear if the mill is going to charge me for the difference.

Paper Coatings: There are many different materials used to coat papers. Some sheets have a clay coating, some have an enamel finish and some have a high-gloss chemical "cast" coating. If a sheet is cast-coated on one side only, it is called C1S (*C one S*). If a sheet is cast-coated on two sides, it is called C2S or (*C two S*).

Paper Grain: Folding against the grain often causes cracking. It is important to know how the grain runs in a sheet you're planning to print on and then fold. Your best source for this information is your paper merchant or your printer.

Paper Weights: This is called the basis weight, and it's the weight of a ream of paper. A ream is 500 sheets.

Different types of papers come in different sizes but the common denominator is the ream. A basis 80 means that 500 sheets 25" x 38" weighs 80 pounds. There are exceptions to this, but for the most part this formula will work for you. Papers are manufactured in Europe that are not standard American weight, but they offer variety and quality. You can profit by knowing about them and their advantages. Call your merchant or mill promotion representative for more information.

Types of Papers

There are different types/grades of papers for different uses, which are often reflected in their names. Coated text and cover are used for the lion's share of four-color printing. Uncoated text and cover are the next up. Bond, book, offset, label, index, and newsprint are other grades used commercially.

Coated Papers: are best suited for higher-quality jobs, and they may be *gloss coated* (usually an enamel coating), dull coated (usually a clay or chemical coating), machine coated (a sheet is made smooth by a blade running over it during the manufacturing process), and *cast-coated* (a high gloss coating used for the highest-quality premium papers) on one or two sides. Printing ink does not soak into a coated sheet as much as it does with an uncoated paper, so coated papers make halftones and color images look richer. Uncoated papers are used for halftones when the designer is trying to achieve a certain effect or look. Coated papers are associated with corporate capability brochures and annual reports. Since coated papers come in several grades and prices, you should not have to shy away from using them. Today, more and more coated papers are recycled, which also lowers their costs. The normal size of the sheet of paper is 23" x 35" or 25" x 38".

Uncoated Papers: Also known as *text*, these papers can be excellent sheets for printing. Some uncoated papers are so smooth that it's hard to tell that they're not coated. (I don't like to refer to these sheets as text, because both coated and uncoated papers come in text and cover weights.) Uncoated papers are manufactured in many textures and colors. They can simulate flannel, linen, corduroy, or other textures. 25" x 38" is the normal sheet size for these papers as well. Uncoated papers seem to be used less by designers using computers, because the output devices for producing layouts, use coated sheets.

Bond: Used for stationery or forms, they take ink well from a typewriter or a pen. Part of this absorbency comes from the paper's rag content, which is the percentage of cotton fiber in a sheet of bond. twenty-five percent or fifty percent is the usual amount added. With the new laser printers, the fine letterhead papers are not as readily used, because they jam up in the printers or soak up the ink. The normal sheet size is 17" x 22", trimmed to 8.5" x 11".

Book: Used, just as the name implies, for books and textbooks, these papers come in antique (rough) or smooth finishes. They also come in many weights; so that a book can be bulked up or down. Normal sheet size is 25" x 38".

Offset papers are similar to the coated and uncoated sheets used in letterpress printing, except that they have sizing added to resist the moisture that occurs in offset printing. The standard sheet size is 25" x 38".

Index papers are stiff and take writing ink well but are less expensive than cover grades. Index papers are used for cards or tabs and are used in place of the more expensive cover stocks. They come in a smooth or vellum (a little rougher) finish. The sheet sizes are 22.5" x 35" or 25.5" x 30".

Newsprint papers, as their name suggests, are used for newspapers. The sheets are not as white as other papers, and ink tends to soak into them. Being relatively inexpensive, newsprint is ideal for the large volumes of paper that modern newspapers need.

There are many great sheets of paper out there. Don't fall into a rut; try them. Your printer is your best consultant on the printability and economics of different papers.

Paper choice can make a major difference in the appearance of your finished job. A dull or plain design can be perked up with an exciting color or texture. But remember one thing, coated and smooth papers make pictures, whether color or black and white, look richer, because the printing ink stands up on the sheet.

I once had a job on press that included a full-color image of an eagle. I had chosen an uncoated white stock. While the printer was in make-ready, he used some coated sheets as waste. To my dismay, the eagle looked much brighter and more vibrant on the coated sheet than it did on the one I had chosen. I've never forgotten this lesson.

This is not to say that halftones and color images can't look good on an uncoated sheet. It only means that you should be aware of the likely effect. When in doubt, call your local paper merchant and ask for the sample room. They can often find an example of the kind of printing you are contemplating, on the sheet you want to use.

Choosing Envelopes

When used, the envelope is an important element of the printed piece. I've heard it said that most business people never see the envelope, because a secretary opens the envelope and throws it into the trash before the recipient gets to see it. Actually, this is more the exception than the rule. Let's face it, most people in middle management don't have secretaries.

My theory is that a good envelope will often save the entire piece from the trash can. How many times has an envelope compelled you to open it? Publisher's Clearing House has certainly learned this secret.

Envelopes come in many standard sizes, mostly in white wove or kraft stocks. There are also envelopes in different colors and textures that are stocked by the paper merchants. If you have a project requiring a special envelope, or if you wish the printing to run across the folds, you can have the envelope converted or manufactured. You should allow more time for this process and budget a little more money. Here again, let the printer be your consultant.

There are wall charts available from envelope companies, showing the different styles and sizes of their envelopes. I suggest getting one of these and taping it on the back of a door that's usually open. A merchant who stocks Strathmore papers should be able to get you an Old Colony envelope wall chart. Old Colony specializes in nothing but envelopes and is the leader in the industry.

If you're in an area without a local merchant, you can contact Old Colony directly at *Old Colony Envelopes, 94 N. Elm Street, Westfield, MA 01086. Phone: 1-800-343-1273.*

Styles of Envelopes

Baronial: Used for formal invitations and announcements, they are usually white. They are identified by their different sizes with an "A" prefix, such as A7 or A8.

Wallet Flap/Bankers Flap: Used for heavy duty purposes, because they will hold materials too bulky for regular envelopes

Commercial: Made in bond or kraft papers, these envelopes are used for everyday business correspondence.

The standard business envelope is the #10, which takes an 8.5" x 11" sheet of paper or standard company stationery. This size is also used for direct mail brochures that are folded from a sheet of paper that is 9" x 12" to a 4" x 9" (6) panel.

Gusseted/Expansion: Used for bulky items, this envelope has a gusset, which is extra paper that folds out to accommodate the contents.

Open-Side/Booklet: The flap of this envelope is on the long side. For instance, if an open-side envelope is 9" x 12", it will open on the 12" side.

Open-End/Catalog: Just the opposite of open-side, this envelope is 9" x 12", opening on the 9" side. The two types can be used interchangeably, depending on your preference.

Self-Sealing: Exactly what their name implies, these envelopes are used mainly for inter-office correspondence or in situations where the materials in the envelope are not confidential.

String with Button and Clasp: Used for inter-office correspondence, both can be sealed and resealed over and over again.

Window: These envelopes have a glassine window so that the addressee's name will show through. Thus the person's name and address, on correspondence or a document, can be used as the mailing address, which avoids duplication of effort, reduces errors, and saves money.

Envelopes can be special. Consider the envelope the introduction to you or your product, and treat it with appropriate care. This way, you're almost sure to make a favorable impression on the recipient.

CHAPTER 10

HOW TO WRITE AN EFFECTIVE PRINTING BID REQUEST AND PURCHASE ORDER

L et's look at what you need in order to buy printing. You already have the first thing, this book. You need a PMS swatch book. PMS is Pantone Matching System. Each color in the swatch book has a number assigned to it. These are like paint chips. PMS colors can fade with age. The yellowing of the paper can also make the colors warmer than they should be. Make sure you always have a fresh book.

You will need paper samples. You can get these from area paper merchants. You will need to create your own Requests For Quotations and purchase orders. I do not suggest using your company's if they are not designed for the graphic arts. Your company's purchasing policies may apply to supplies they buy in general, and that will confuse the printer as well as distract from your intent.

If you decide that the printing negatives belong to your company, you should make note of this on your RFQ and PO. The Printing Trade Customs say the negatives are the property of the printer. Also, you may wish to include in your PO that you will not pay for over runs and you will not accept under runs. You can describe how you want your job packaged and delivered. Purchase orders should be at least a two-part form so you will have a copy after one is sent to the printer. You will also need a printing RFQ form. The obvious is true. The bigger the project the more complex the RFQ and PO has to be. The sample RFQ on the next page is typical.

The Request For Quotation (RFQ)

The Request For Quotation is the invitation for the printer or designer to submit a fixed price for a specific project. This should not be confused with an estimate. An estimate is a loose guess as to what a job will cost. You want a well thought-out bid.

With this in mind, you want to make sure your specifications are as tight as possible and all points are covered. You can always use one of your printers as a sounding board by submitting a draft to them before you send out the formal RFQ.

The Purchase Order

A purchase order can be a simple note, but it is only effective if you retain a copy for your file. If there's a dispute, you may find that your original note has mysteriously disappeared leaving you with no records.

If you are working for an advertising agency, you may want to have the printing billed directly to your client. If that's the case, you will probably provide print management and bill your client for your time. In that the case, you may want to call your purchase order a "Start Order." The information will be the same, but you are indicating to the printer that you are not buying those services.

If you are not buying the printing, you may be asked by the printer to have your client fill out a credit application.

Printing RFQ

XYZ Corporation
100 Xenia Drive
Anytown, USA 10000

(212) 555-4444

To: Acme Printing Co. Inc.

From: XYZ Corporation

Re: Jane Smith

Date: 8/7/1999

This is a request for a quotation for the printing of the XYZ Corporation Capabilities Brochure. Please fax your quote to Jane Smith, Project Director, at fax # (212) 555-5555 and mail hard copy.

Size: 8.5" x 11" folded

Colors: Two PMS colors with dull spot varnish

No. Pages: 16 plus cover

Binds: Saddle stitched on the 11" side

Stock: LOE Dull 80lb Cover and LOE Gloss 100lb Text

Quantity: 5,000 Copies

Copy: QuarkXPress 3.2 disk w/ 300 DPI Proofs

Due date: 10/11/99

Deliver to: XYZ Corporation

Invoice: XYZ Corporation

Quote: $ _____

All negatives belong to the XYZ Corporation. The XYZ Corporation will not pay for over runs and will not accept under runs unless authorized by an officer of the company.

Completion of a credit application for the printer is standard procedure, so you may want to have this done early in the production process. If the job is time sensitive and has to go to the printer before your client can fill out the credit form, you can guarantee the project through your own company. This should only be done if your client has a good credit history with your company.

If your printing specifications change, I recommend preparing an update or revised PO with a new date. It's up to you to cover your bases. It is easier for you to detail your own project and more important for you to be able to track your project. It is very important that you set up a job numbering system. These numbers are your only method of tracking invoices. The PO number is important as it distinguishes what service and vendor you are using, but the job number is your record of the entire project. Under that one number you may have many purchase orders.

Job numbers are also job jackets. It is a good idea to use a folder to hold all of the purchase orders, text drafts etc. If you are part of a large company, you can set up job jackets for your in-house clients under a separate numbering system. If they have phone extensions, you can use those numbers.

The Purchase Order is best used if it is introduced at the beginning of a project. This is especially true if the printer or the designer has their own trade customs and presents them before you establish your own ground rules. Life is one long string of negotiations, and with most negotiations there is a closing with a signed agreement. If your purchase order is the only signed agreement, you stand a good chance of prevailing. Even if the only signature present is your own.

The samples I have shown are specifically designed for a print project. Purchase orders are for every purchase.

Printing Purchase Order

XYZ Corporation
100 Xenia Drive
Anytown, USA 10000

PO #1000
Job #2000

(212) 555-4444

To: Acme Printing Co. Inc.

From: XYZ Corporation

Re: Jane Smith

Date: 8/7/1999

This is a purchase order for the printing of the XYZ Corporation Capabilities Brochure. The job number and purchase order number must appear on all invoices. The specifications are as follows:

Size: 8.5" x 11" folded

Colors: Two PMS colors with dull spot varnish

Pages: 16 plus cover

Binds: Saddle stitched on the 11" side

Stock: LOE Dull 80lb Cover and LOE Gloss 100lb Text

Qty: 5,000 Copies

Copy: 3.2 QuarkXPress disk w/ 300 DPI Proofs

Due: 10/11/99

Deliver: XYZ Corporation

Invoice: XYZ Corporation

Quote: $10,000.00

All disks and copy must be returned to XYZ Corporation. All negatives belong to the XYZ Corporation. The XYZ Corporation will not pay for over runs and will not accept under runs unless authorized by an officer of the company.

For the XYZ Corporation   Date

Design Purchase Order

XYZ Corporation   PO #1000
100 Xenia Drive   Job#2000
Anytown, USA 10000

(212) 555-4444

To: Creative Design Services, Inc.

From: XYZ Corporation

Re: Jane Smith

Date: 7/15/1999

This is a purchase order for the layout and design production of the XYZ Corporation Capabilities Brochure. The job number and purchase order number must appear on all invoices. The specifications are as follows:

The Size is 8.5" x 11" folded, colors are two PMS colors with four color process and a dull spot varnish, 16 pages plus cover, saddle stitched on the 11" side, stock to be determined. Quantity is 5,000 copies, text will be furnished as Word Perfect Disk. Deliver disk to XYZ Corporation. Estimate is $3,000.00

All deliveries to the XYZ Corporation will use the company's courier. Letters of Transmittal must accompany any materials sent to XYZ Corporation.

_____

For the XYZ Corporation   Date

Vendors and your Purchase Order

It is smart to make sure each vendor is aware of your purchase order system. They should be aware, that unless they reference your job number and your purchase order number within each of their invoices, they might not get paid.

This is serious business and you cannot take it lightly. Your exposure, when buying big ticket items like printing, can be your professional demise, if you're not careful.

If your changes run
more than 10% of the cost of the
initial work, you're making too many
changes.

It is also important for you to issue a new purchase order every time you send a vendor an update (change order). This references those changes, so you know what your changes cost you. If your changes run more than ten percent of the cost of the initial work, you're making too many changes.

If you are buying typography, this means you are not proofing your copy before it is set. It can also mean your internal system is not efficient. For instance, you receive a typed manuscript from someone within your organization to send to a graphic designer. You send it to the designer and you receive page proofs back. Next, you give the page proofs back to the person who gave you the manuscript. They in turn show it to their boss who makes changes. They send the page proofs back to you with the new changes. You then fill out another purchase order and send everything back to the designer.

If they had their boss sign-off on the original manu-script, the changes would be minimal. This may be beyond your control, and part of company politics, so be careful. Don't criticize, suggest.

Managing Your Department & Promoting Your Company

You wear many hats, so wear them with style.

CHAPTER 11

HOW TO SET UP A CHARGE-BACK SYSTEM IN YOUR COMPANY

Charge-backs give companies and organizations a way of attaching a monetary value to internal services rendered. This is a useful arrangement, but it may become your nemesis if your not careful. You need to guard against elaborate formulas which are not necessarily good just because they are complicated. The more complicated these systems are, the more likely it is that they will be abused or disbanded.

Centralization

Charge-backs are a function of centralization, when specific areas within a company perform services for the rest of the company. An example of this is the Printing and Publications Division which purchases all outside printing for the company. The other divisions use this group exclusively, and do not buy any printing themselves. If run correctly, this system can be very efficient, letting one group put all of its energies and expertise into one activity, and restricting all other personnel from issuing printing purchase orders for printing services.

Centralization starts to break down as soon as there are exceptions. For example, problems arise when high paid executives get involved in small printing projects even though they had a perfectly capable printing division.

Earlier, I mentioned abuse. Centralization can also give purchasing power to an individual who uses that power to get kick-backs. The vendor or printer is told that if they would like to do business with the company, this certain individual expects a percentage. There are all kinds of nice terms for this. Some call it a "finders fee," others call it a commission. I call it a kick-back. That's not a pretty term nor is the procedure, in my opinion, an honest one.

I was once asked by a printing broker, who had introduced me to a new client, to give him a finders fee every time the client used my company (whether or not the broker was involved in the project). I told him that it was fine with me, but I would have to let the client know, because I would have to add that amount to the bill. I told him that my margin of profit wasn't large enough to cover his kick-back, and he immediately backed off.

Decentralization

Decentralization is used by companies and organizations that want each area of the company to act independently from the others. In this way, these areas compete with each other to achieve greater profits, thus causing the company as a whole to be more profitable.

In theory, this can work if the areas have properly trained personnel within them. Most people are good at the specific tasks they were trained for. This does not mean they should be purchasing agents. Printing and graphic design are technical processes that require full attention.

If your job is to buy design and/or printing, and that is all that you do, you probably are in a centralized environment. If you have other people working with or for you, you may be asked to justify your existence monetarily.

You are a Profit Center

Your company has asked you to set up an internal billing system, so that they can charge the other departments for your services. It doesn't matter if you are a marketing department copywriter, an in-house graphic designer, or a print buyer. The end-result is they are setting a price for your services.

Some companies use unnecessarily complicated systems to establish these values, but a realistic and fairly simple one is outlined.

The System

First, you must affix an hourly rate to your department's labor. This can be one rate for everyone, or it can be an individual rate for each person. You can even use the hourly rates to determine a cost by project.

To determine an individual's hourly rate, simply multiply their actual hourly rate by four. If a person is making $30,000 a year, that person's hourly rate is $15. The billable rate is $15 x 4 = $60 per hour. This takes into consideration their benefits, and overhead, such as rent, phones, supplies, administrative personnel etc. This type of formula is used by lawyers and accountants. You can vary the ratio depending on where company is located. Obviously the east and west coasts are going to be higher, so you might use 4.5 for New York and 3.5 for a more rural area.

The individual, billable hourly rates are based on peoples salaries. This presupposes that the more a person is paid, the more, you can bill for that person's time. It should also mean that that person is capable of working faster and giving more value to his or her hourly rate.

To keep track of each person's billable time, you need a system. Each project within your department probably has a number already assigned to it. If not, start a numbering system, and use the simplest workable way to assign client and job numbers to individual projects. As mentioned earlier, the client's number could be his or her phone extension. This makes it simple to contact them, and guarantees there will be no duplicates. As for the individual job numbers, you could start with the number 1 or 1,000. The client and job should then be used on any purchase order or in-house invoice.

Next, you should design a time sheet for each person to keep up daily. I've tried weekly, but people have a tendency to wait until the end of the week to fill them out. At that point, they are just guessing.

The time sheet on the opposite page is very simple, but adequate. You could make your codes letter abbreviations for services, like *CM* for Client Meeting or *R* for Research. If the hourly rate for the person in the example is $60, the day's work is worth $480.

When the time sheet is turned in, someone must enter the hours and codes into a data bank, to be used to generate an invoice. There are simple programs that can be adapted to run this system. A more sophisticated approach is to network everyone into a central system, so that the times and codes are immediately posted to each project electronically.

If you want to reduce the charge-back system to its simplest form, you could average out the time used by individuals to complete a project, and apply a total figure based on the size and scope of the job. However, this only works accurately if you have a constant repetition of similar projects. This would never be practical in a commercial environment. Real dollars must be attached to efficiency and captured accurately.

Time Sheet

XYZ Corporation

Name: Jane Doe
Date: 8/7/99

Job #	Hours	Code
1000	2.5	Writing
1001	.5	Editing
1003	1.0	Client Meeting
1008	.5	Research
1015	.5	Print Management
1001	.25	Print Management
1028	.5	Editing
1014	1.0	Research
1000	.5	Writing
1003	.25	Overhead
1028	.5	Editing
Total	**8.0**	

Markups

When you or your department buys an outside product or service, you should mark up the cost when passing it along to another department. twenty percent is the normal markup. This is for the labor in handling the costs, not the project. Do not include services within the mark up. Commercial companies don't. This is a normal way of doing business internally as well as externally. This may be a stumbling block when you present your plan for charge-backs. Most corporate people have no real grasp of how business is conducted outside their company. In fact, they don't really know how to gauge their own hourly worth. Perhaps because they have never been forced to think in terms of overall economics, most people take their own overhead costs for granted. They don't see themselves as part of the profit-and-loss equation of the company as a whole.

But a successful company needs to be profitable on every level, with each employee being regarded as a profit center, and this is the real reason for charge-backs. This system places a monetary value on everyone's contribution to the bottom line, and prevents a potential "profit center" from becoming a drain on the rest of the company's resources.

Be Prepared

On the other hand, you and your department will have to justify your charge-backs, just as your vendors have to justify their invoices that they send to you. Charge-backs are likely to be as unpopular with your in-house clients as they are a pain in the neck for you, and you must expect some grief if you or your people take "too much time" on a project. Next to their own money, nothing is as precious as your client's own internal budget.

CHAPTER 12

HOW TO CREATE A GRAPHICS STANDARDS PROGRAM

G raphic standards are important from several standpoints. Above all, your company's visual personality is its logo and logotype. The better the graphic portrayal the more impact your company has in its competitive playing field. Earlier, we talked about corporate identity and how the seventies saw companies jump on the graphic standards bandwagon. This was not a fluke or fashionable whim. Good graphics affect everyone within a company. Salespeople feel pride when their business cards and stationery have visual impact and so do other employees.

The Logo

To initiate graphic standards, you must have a strong and distinctive logo. This is the foundation; if the logo is weak, your standards will not strengthen it. If you only have enough money budgeted for a redesign of your current logo, do it now and don't worry about a full set of standards until later.

As soon as you have the new logo, you should incorporate it into high visibility areas of the company, such as signage, stationery, and the like. Then gradually phase it in to everything else by which your company can be identified.

This means paying attention even to little things like forms.

Let's talk about corporate graphics. What is the corporate symbol/logo? The symbol is the Jolly Green Giant, the Golden Arches, the Westinghouse *W,* or the Mercedes Star. What is the signature/logotype? They are the words and the typestyles naming these products and services. Example are: the words Bell Atlantic with the Bell symbol, the word Texaco with the red *T,* and the word Apple with the apple symbol.

What are Graphic Standards?

Graphic standards are the guidelines for the use of the official company logo and logotype on everything from stationery to signage. The standards are usually published in the form of a manual, which may be anything from a saddle stitched brochure or an elaborate three-ring binder.

Companies use their graphic standards to ensure that people within the company will adhere to the design formats created for the company. So why official standards? Just stick with what was designed. This sounds simple and may work fine in the beginning. But later, new people in the company may decide to place their personal imprint on collateral materials by changing the original designs.

Printers may also inadvertently change things when reprinting stationery or business cards, unless they have a graphic standard manual to refer to. Be generous with your manuals.

I once had a client whose business cards were displayed in a little plexiglass holder on his desk. I noticed that the gray ink on the cards was so pale that it was barely readable. Since I had designed his cards, I knew something was wrong. I learned that the printer had used the wrong ink in the second reprint, and subsequent reprints were getting lighter and lighter. If there had been written standards available to the printer, this mistake probably would never have occurred. Also, if the client had sent a sample business card that was acceptable with the purchase order, the printer would probaly caught the error.

Starting the Graphic Standards Process

The first thing you need is a graphic designer. If your company already has a strong logo, you should consider using the designer of that mark for the development of the complete set of standards, unless your company ceased doing business with this designer for some reason or another; so check this out first. There is also another possibility that would have a bearing on this project.

Does the designer of the logo have any experience with total graphic standards? If not, start interviewing designers who have. This is a complex process that requires professional input. If you have no stable of graphic designers, use the networking method. Call local companies that have good graphics. Talk to their corporate communications people, and find out who they have used. Most likely they'll be flattered and happy to share the designer's name with you. This only works if these people are not competitors. Next, invite the designer or designers to submit a proposal.

Your RFP should state all of your objectives as clearly as possible. An outline for the contents of the graphic standards manual is a good place to begin. Such a manual, as detailed below, will contain all of the design solutions for your corporate materials, which should give you a handle on your entire budget for design. In addition, you could also use this outline to develop printing specifications for getting estimates on print production. Most companies order too few manuals and then have be very discrimnitory as to who gets a copy. Don't make this same mistake. The number of manuals printed, when under one-hundred copies, is minimal in the per-unit cost.

The Graphic Standards Manual Contents

The manual must be all inclusive. Whatever you leave out today, could become tomorrow's graphic design nightmare. Since each company is different, you may not need everything here, or you may need some additional design guidelines, but this basic outline will get you started.

Cover: This should highlight the logo and say exactly what the manual is, such as: *ABC Corporation Graphic Standards Manual.*

Contents: The contents simply lists the sections in the manual. You may not need this if you use tabs to separate the sections. Tabs can be restrictive if you plan to update or change the manual later. You may want to label the tabs with numbers or letters. This way you can change the categories within the tabs. This may not seem necessary now, but you may be glad you did it after you've lived with the manual for awhile.

1. Corporate Symbol and Signature: This section shows the logo and logotype or symbol and signature shown in its entirety as a complimentary unit.

> *A. Introduction.* This page explains the reason for the symbol and signature, its unique qualities and acceptable color/colors. This also gives the rationale behind the "standards."

> *B. The Corporate Symbol.* The symbol/logo is shown on a quarter inch grid in an approximately 7" x 7" size. This gives the exact proportions for recreating the symbol. This is also a guide for sign painters.

> *C. The Symbol and Signature.* This illustrates the company's name with the logo. Here the proportions are shown as well as special colors.

D. The Symbol and Signature (Unacceptable Use). The logo and logotype are shown in different colors, shapes and proportions that are incorrect. This is a "Don't Ever Do This!" page.

E. Corporate Colors. This page shows the correct ink color/colors for the symbol and/or the signature. Complimentary colors that work well with the official color combination can also be shown on this page

F. Corporate Typography. These are examples of the company's official typefaces. Most corporations have two faces, a sans serif and a serif.

2. Reproduction Sheets: This section shows the symbol and signature as they should appear in various sizes and configurations. These pages are meant to be used for reproduction and are always printed in black on a white field.

A. Repro Sheet 1. This sheet may show a flush left or flush right configuration of the symbol and signature.

B. Repro Sheet 2. This sheet is a variation of the preceding one, with a centered or other alternate version of the symbol and signature.

3. Corporate Stationery and Business Papers: The formats for the collateral materials are shown in this section.

A. The Corporate Letterhead. This page shows the official letterhead with the typefaces and placement of all elements.

B. The Second Sheet. This sheet is optional and is only shown if there is some design element on it.

C. The Business Envelope. The corporation may have several different envelopes. These are shown on this page with their correct type and symbol layouts.

D. The Business Card. The official business card format is illustrated on this page. Generally the card is shown actual size.

E. The Mailing Label. The label is an important element within the stationery system. The design format is shown actual size.

F. The Business Forms. Business forms are another communication element seen by your business public. The design of your forms should be shown here.

4. Corporate Publications: This section addresses the design of corporate literature.

A. The Corporate Newsletter. This communication vehicle should be friendly and inviting but it should also project the same graphic image as other company materials. This is especially true if the newsletter is sent to clients/customers.

B. The Corporate Marketing Brochure. This type of brochure may or may not fall under a strict graphic standards guideline. You may wish to show only how the symbol and signature are used, or you might want a strict set of typographical guidelines to govern the design of these brochures

C. Marketing and Speciality Materials. If the corporation produces promotional items like coffee mugs, tee shirts, etc., the graphic standards may allow the symbol without the signature to appear on the item if the entire symbol and signature appear somewhere else.

5. Signage/Environmental Graphics: These pages show the authorized ways of designing corporate signage both internal an external. This is an important part of the company's look.

A. Building Signage. If your company has internal or external signage, you need to use your graphic standards system to link these together visually.

B. Vehicle Signage. If your company has a corporate fleet of trucks, cars etc., a guide for the application of the corporate symbol and signature should be clearly illustrated here.

There are many other sections you may be able to add to the manual and some you can subtract. Your company may specialize in something like mortgage banking, for which these standards could be overkill. But you might also be working for a major industrial company, and need much more detailed graphic standards than we can present here.

The Next Step

You've outlined your graphic standards manual, and now you're ready for the next stage of the process.

After selecting the designer, as discussed above, hold a meeting to establish all of the parameters of the project. This includes your designer's understanding of the the RFP, their understanding of the outline of the manual, and their game plan for remaining within the budget.

You should be prepared for several review meetings to determine the political ramifications of design decisions. For instance, only you may know that a certain individual will be insulted by their incorrect title on a proof.

It's up to you to oversee the design process closely.

CHAPTER 13

HOW TO EFFECTIVELY PROMOTE YOUR COMPANY

Promotion is an art form and many fine books have been written on the subject. Whether you work for a Fortune 500 company or a small law firm, promotion can help a company survive. Here, I'll use my own experience to highlight some of the basics.

My lawyer once invited me to a partners' dinner meeting, to discuss his firm's new marketing approach. This was explained to me as a monthly meeting of the partners, to plan strategies. I thought that I would be part of a discussion on marketing the law firm to the public.

Wrong! After dinner I was introduced as the person who would now give the partners a seminar on the new marketing plan for their firm.

Not wanting to embarrass my host, I decided to wing it. First, I told the partners that it was their individual responsibility to sell for the firm, not by cold-calling but by joining the Rotary Club, the Chamber of Commerce, and other community organizations.

Next, they needed a PR plan. This meant someone had to be in charge of sending out press releases whenever something newsworthy happened in the firm.

I told them that they also needed a simple brochure that was nothing more than an extension of their business card. This brochure would fit in a standard business envelope and each partner's bio would be on a single sheet, and placed in a pocket in the back of the brochure.

I then talked about a simple but catchy series of ads. These ads would be very general, simply promoting the law firm as a reputable and multi-talented group of partners versus a group of "ambulance chasers."

Everything I said was based on common sense. These ideas weren't new, except for the ads.

Last but not least, I remembered a large clock on their reception area wall. I couldn't resist an experiment. I told them that any of them could run a little late, some more than others. The clock was an unnecessary reminder, to those waiting in the reception area, of just how late they were running. After all, it takes a conscious effort to look at a watch versus just looking up from a magazine at a wall clock.

I was given a hearty round of applause for my little common sense approach to marketing. Two weeks later, I was in my lawyer's office reception area. There was a big pale spot on the wall above the receptionist. I asked, "What had happened to the clock?"

She replied, "I'm not really sure. About two weeks ago the partners came in one morning and the next thing I knew, the clock was gone."

I smiled to myself.

Maketing is Necessity

Marketing is a series of efforts to promote your company. The only difference between the the law firm and your company is your imagination or knowledge. Don't bite off more than you can chew, but don't be so sure you can't bite off quite a bit. You are marketing your company all of the time. Remember the lawyers? I asked a person in my firm, what they would've done if asked to come up with an instant marketing seminar. I was hoping for another solution, but I got a blunt answer, "I would've thrown-up!"

Marketing is only effective when it's used. I've been to many good seminars on the "How To" of marketing, and I've seen others forget everything they paid money to learn, as soon as they got back to their office. *No* game plan will guarantee *no* results. Marketing is work, but you can see results.

Let's Look at You and Your Company

Some companies already have a public relations program in place. Look around at yours and don't be too quick to offer suggestions until you thoroughly understand what has been done in the past and have decided what you want to do. I have seen many a shot from the hip come back as a ricochet into the heart. This can be a killer for future projects.

Usually a public relations program had an author. Find out if that author is still around. You don't need surprises if that person is now above you.

First, Clean House

The best way to get your company's PR juices flowing, is to hold an open house. This is a great way to promote your company and to get the facilities cleaned up. I've even used this as a deadline to have a corporate brochure printed.

Don't take the open house lightly. There should be a theme. I know of one firm that holds a Valentine's Day. After all, February is a partyless month. You can usually negotiate a good deal with a caterer. You can use the open house to announce a new product or service, an anniversary, or any other excuse to invite clients to your offices.

The decorating done for an open house, is usually permanent and will last the rest of the year.

Corporate Brochure

Every company needs a brochure. In many parts of the world, business people used to exchange business cards whenever they would meet. Now a company brochure is considered the best way to introduce yourself to the world.

Your company brochure doesn't have to be fancy. It doesn't have to be expensive. But it had better be good. In an information age, such as ours, people are inundated with good graphics and good brochures. The difference between conservative and mundane is a fine line. Often good design is the best differential for making your message stand out in the crowd.

Maybe your company has an internal design group that they want you to use. Or maybe you are the internal designer. I advise against designing a piece of this magnitude in-house. There's a rule that I feel is very valid, if the piece to be designed is going to be used internally, design it internally. If it is going to be used outside the company, have an outside design firm design it. Of course this can change if your company is very large and has thousands of employees. If that's the case, you may want to have that piece designed by an outside designer as well.

If your corporate brochure is going to be used by salespeople, you will need to hire a writer as well as a designer. Don't expect the writing to be a snap either. This is where someone must get to know and understand your company thoroughly. Every company says they're different from their competition, but when most are pressed, they can't say why. How can they expect a writer to verbalize what management can't.

Don't rely on copy to tell your company's story. You have less than ten seconds to hook most of the people who will receive your brochure. Color, photography, or illustrations will grab faster than any words. Words are important, but you need a reader first.

Executive Biographies

Update your executives' biographies, and make them more exciting. I like to call these "Profiles." You can really spice them up as much as possible. There is no reason why someone's obituary should be more exciting than their biography was when they were alive.

> *There is no reason why someone's obituary should be more exciting than their biography was when they were alive.*

Most people have a hard time writing their own biography or profile. Their professional credentials take on a very routine tone. It's not because they have poor credentials. On the contrary, they could be brilliant, but it is always hard to blow one's own horn. People are usually shy when writing about themselves. Get a professional writer to do this.

There's an art to writing a good profile. For example, one of my employees had only a little professional experience prior to working for me.

I had to really work on her profile to give her credibility. I couldn't lie. She was good and clearly someone who was very talented, despite her lack of experience. She was born in Europe and I decided to make this a plus. I played on her strengths and her recent successes while working on projects in my studio. She is very talented and deserved a good biography. The result is shown on the next page.

XYZ Corporation
Biographical Profile

Jane Smith
Senior Designer

Ms. Smith is a senior designer at the XYZ Corporation. Whether she is directing a special project or participating as a key member of a design team, Ms. Smith offers an array of special talents. She is highly skilled in illustration and photography, and has a thorough knowledge of the complex Macintosh programs which XYZ utilizes.

Ms. Smith has worked with national account, bringing a unique European flair to everyday design problems. She is proficient in her knowledge of all aspects of the prepress process and has worked with the latest prepress technologies.

Prior to joining the XYZ Corporation, Ms. Smith was a designer at Electric Images in New York. Before that, she freelanced for Studio XL in New Jersey, and also freelanced for Jones, Doe & Smith in Connecticut.

Ms. Smith graduated with honors and a BFA from The University of Buffalo, College of Art and Design. She also studied at the Swiss School of Design in Basel, Switzerland and as well The University of Rome in Italy.

Ms. Smith is fluent in both French and Italian.

The All-Important Press Release

The press release is an excellent way to blow your company's horn. First, collect the names and addresses of editors and publications in which you want to have your releases published. And always remember that a press release has to feature newsworthy information. It can announce a person's promotion or some new product breakthrough, it can't sell. And I can't emphasize this strongly enough.

The structure of a typical press release is an inverted triangle, with the bulk of information at the top and the least important at the bottom. That way, the editor can chop it off at the end of any paragraph, without losing vital information. Here is an example.

XYZ Corporation Press Release

For Immediate Release:

Washington, D.C. The XYZ Corporation announces a breakthrough in photo retouching. The development of XYZ Interactive Software offers an electronic retouching package equal to those of the large prepress systems costing hundreds of thousands more.

XYZ Corporation spokesman, John Smith, says the breakthrough will give small design studios the capability of competing with the large prepress labs.

The software uses a sophisticated paint system, with a Macintosh 840 Quadra. The software cost is approximately $10,000 and a complete workstation is double that amount.

For further information contact Jane Doe at: (202) 555-5555

Please note that the press release, on the previous page, comes dangerously close to selling and probably would only be picked up by trade publications.

I've found it very helpful to gather together a list of publications, the names of their editors, and addresses. I divided the list into specific areas of interest. The "master list" contained all of the publications. "List A" contained high tech publications for product announcements, and "list B" contained general interest publications for personnel announcements and other general company news.

The Map

If your company is in a remote area, such as an industrial park, develop a postcard-size map for prospective visitors. The map can be very simple but clear; everyone in the company should be encouraged to use it. When designing the map, make sure it will fit in a standard business envelope or it can be used as a self mailer.

Advertising

If your company is large, it probably has an advertising agency working for it, but this area is often overlooked by small companies.

If your company doesn't have an agency but it does have a budget, work up a game plan. Many small companies find it profitable to advertise in the yellow pages, and they will help you with the layout and design of your ad or ads.

Many companies also spend time and money advertising in trade publications. Since these are read only by their competitors, this practice has never made sense to me.

You can create simple ads, a graphic designer is all that you need. You can be the writer, and place the ads yourself, remembering that the secret to successful advertising is frequency. It does no good to run an ad once and then pull it.

The public is very busy, and you have to "hit them over the head" by running your ad numerous times to get their attention.

The Clock

Don't forget the clock in your company's reception area. Get rid of it now. This may have been a second thought in my marketing seminar, but it was a valid observation and it could make your visitors a lot happier, as well as enhance your total promotional effort.

The Marketing Consultant

Marketing is a company effort. Everyone counts. If need be, hire a marketing consultant. It is not so much that they know more than you do, but that your voice may be falling on management's deaf ears. It's very true that we assign more worth to something we pay for. An example of this, is a case close to home.

I asked an editor friend of mine to read this book, and to feel free to use her infamous red pen. She did and my manuscript was a sea of red marks. I decided to make only limited changes. She had added numerous commas, and I questioned almost all of them.

It was agreed upon by both of us up front, that I would recieve a bill for her sevices. When I got her bill a few days later, I looked at her work quite differently. I made every single correction that she had marked. After all, I paid for all of those commas.

It has often been said that an outside voice is listened to by management, because an insider must be part of the problem. Whether it's true or not, it is a fact that can't be ignored. So go with the flow. Hire a consultant who shares your views. This is where networking can be effective. You can meet the consultants who you want to work with later.

What If There's No Budget for Marketing

If this is the case in your company, you'll have to get creative. Clip competitor's advertisements. Go to industry trade shows and pick up competitor's brochures and other handouts. Collect good examples of competitor's stationery and logos.

Now it's time to sit down with management. Show them what the competion is doing and discuss ways of moving funds from one budget to another. Namely, to yours. Have as many books on marketing that you can find. The public library is a good source.

There are things that don't require much money. The press releases and the employee biographies require little money. You may want to hire a professional writer, but in the case of the bios, it will be a one time expense. The map can be one color and inexpensive to print, but I would suggest that you pay a graphic designer to make it simple and attractive.

TERMS AND TRADE CUSTOMS

No longer is it *business as usual*.

CHAPTER 14

BUSINESS TERMS COMMONLY USED IN THE GRAPHIC ARTS

The following terms are meant to help you understand words that may be thrown around while you are negotiating with a designer, photographer, printer, etc. You may know most of these words and this might seem silly, but this section may just reaffirm and further clarify what you thought you knew.

Your suppliers have an advantage. They are in business to survive, and the terms they use are precise. They cannot afford misunderstandings or mistakes that could kill their companies. By the same token, you must realize exactly what is being said to you, verbally or in writing. No good business person wants to surprise his client, at the end of a project, with an invoice full of unexpected charges. But it's "buyer beware," and you need to know as much as you can. And remember, what you don't understand, ask. These suppliers are working for you.

The following terms are presented because they relate directly to you, and to the seller of graphic arts products and services. Other terms are not listed because they are obscure, or not common to the graphic arts industry.

Accounts Payable is the money owed by a company to a creditor for goods or services purchased.

Accounts Receivable is the money owed to a company for work performed and invoices issued. Your invoices from them are their receivables.

Aging is the money owed to a company, noted by the length of time it has been outstanding. This is measured in 30, 60, 90, or 120-day increments. Aging is very important to banks when considering a loan for a company.

Alterations are changes you make to work completed correctly by your supplier. This is the one area you must try to control, because it's probably your company's greatest area of wasted money. The industry average for alteration is said to be ten percent. Don't believe it. It's really more like thirty to forty percent.

Arbitration is settling a dispute through an individual or a panel, rather than in a court of law. If both parties can agree on this method, they will save legal fees and court costs.

Blueline is the last proof, and must be considered sacred. The blueline is probably one of the most important documents you'll ever sign. This proof is made from the final negatives that will be used to make the actual printing plates, and that's why blueline corrections are so expensive. Use your other proofing stages carefully.

BPA or **Blanket Purchase Agreement**, is an open or standing purchase order for an amount of money you can spend with a supplier. BPAs are used for multiple projects during a given time frame. For instance, a BPA for ninety days for $20,000 to a supplier means you can spend the $20,000 on different projects for ninety days. Every company qualifies service companies differently, so learn about your company's procedures from your accounts payable staff. It's best to do some research on how much you'll need alloted for your projects. It's always harder to go back to the well, if you run short.

BPO or **Blanket Purchase Order**, is the same as a Blanket Purchase Agreement. Some companies use one term, some use the other.

Brokering is when someone buys a good or service and resells it to another. A service charge is usually added to the cost, and this mark-up is the broker's profit.

Cash Flow is the coming and going of money that every business experiences. It is the constant cycle of invoicing, being paid, paying out cash to suppliers, and making payroll. Interruptions in cash flow will cause companies to borrow money.

Change Orders, another term for alterations, are changes made to existing work or proofs. They are billable, just like other alterations, and you can control them.

Comp Time is hours given as time off for hours worked as overtime. Companies paying comp time should not bill more than their normal hourly rate for overtime situations.

Contract is a written agreement between two parties, outlining the responsibilities of each. A contract can be no more than a memo from one party to the next, spelling out the terms of the agreement. If the recipient does not respond, then the party sending the memo is presumed to be correct. You can create your own "paper trail" and protect yourself from liabilities that your supplier assumes you will accept. This is important, because virtually all business is conducted on the basis of contract in our society.

Cost Per M is cost per thousand. When asking for a printing estimate or quotation over 5,000 copies, it pays to ask for a price for additional thousands at the time of the run.

Estimate is a best-guess calculation of what a good or service will cost. An estimate is not necessarily a bottom-line cost. It is not a quotation or a formal proposal.

FOB or **Freight On Board** is used to specify location of delivery, such as F.O.B. Detroit.

Indemnification is protection from legal reprisal. If you agree to someone's indemnification in a situation, you are agreeing that they are not liable in that situation. In addition, there are certain situations where an individual is automatically indemnified. For instance: if a graphic designer designs a logo for your company and another designer creates the same logo at the same time for another company, your designer is not liable for any lawsuits stemming from that design, because your designer was acting on good faith and unknowingly created the same logo. Your best protection is to start the trademark registration process as soon as possible.

Invoice is a bill for a specific product or service, and only one invoice is issued. Most companies pay invoices only, and never statements. Unpaid invoices will appear on monthly statements, and interest may be charged against the unpaid balance. If you have a dispute over an invoice, you should pay any portion not in dispute, immediately. Any dispute should be called to the seller's attention, prior to the invoice becoming past due.

Letter of Intent is a letter defining the terms of an agreement. It can be from a supplier to you or from you to a supplier. When there is no contract, this is the next best thing. And if you generate the letter, you can make sure you are fully protected. Always respond to a letter of intent, in writing, if the letter to you is not correct. A verbal response can easily be forgotten at a crucial, later date.

Liability in business means exposure to legal action or financial responsibility. It is up to you to understand each facet of the graphic arts process affecting you. Ignorance is not protection, and every letter, memo, or other written document decreases your liability. You can transfer liability in the beginning, but when it's too late, you can be hung with it.

Mark-up is a handling charge. Mark-ups can be any amount added to a good or service bought by a supplier for you. Usually mark-ups do not include any service by the a designer or broker, so you can save money by having a supplier, such as a printer, bill you direct.

Out Of Pocket Expenses are costs to your designer, photographer, or printer in addition to their labor. These suppliers will often give a flat fee for their services plus out of pocket expenses. This can be tricky so get a written definition of what "out of pocket expenses" really means. For instance, you don't want to buy someone a car so he can travel on your behalf!

PEs or **Printer's Errors** are errors made by your supplier. They are often noted as PEs so that you won't be charged for them. However, if there are just a few PEs and many changes made by your company, it will be very hard for the supplier to delineate or separate his PEs from your alterations.

Photo Art Direction is the time a designer spends supervising photography and reviewing proofs. Here again, it is better to have the photography billed directly to you and for the designer only to bill you for the time he or she is needed to perform art direction.

Print Management is the time a designer spends working with a printer. Creating a schedule, providing specifications, checking proofs, and press inspecting are all part of print management.

Printing Overrun is when a printer runs more copies than you have ordered. Check with the printer as to your liability in such an instance, because some printers will charge for the excess. Make sure you understand the printer's terms and conditions. You do have the opportunity of dictating your own terms, specifically that you will not pay for overage, in your purchase order.

Printing Underrun is a run that is short. The printer may say in their terms and conditions of sale that a percentage of underage is acceptable. Here again, as the client, you can disagree in your purchase order.

Proposal is a fixed-price bid for a good or service. Usually proposals will contain: a capability statement showing the suppliers' credentials; a technical proposal stating how the supplier intends to accomplish the project goals; resumes of key individuals who will work on the project: cost proposal; and references with phone numbers.

Registered Trademark is a logo or logotype that has been registered through the U.S. Patent and Trademark Office. An *R* in a circle signifies that the trademark has been registered. If you are in a position within your company to recommend registering your company's logo, I strongly urge you to do so. Remember indemnification; the first company to initiate registration has the best chance of the design's survival as his own property.

RFP or **Request For Proposal** is usually a form sent to suppliers, inviting them to submit a proposal on a specific project. Be sure to note on the RFP that it is not a purchase order. Make sure your specifications and project goals are clear. Don't use ambiguous language.

RFQ or **Request For Quotation** serves the same purpose as an RFP.

Search is the work you perform prior to submitting a logo or logotype for formal registration. The Patent and

Trademark Office will help you if you wish to try to do this yourself, but my advice is to let a lawyer take this step.

Servicemark is used when the logo or logotype represents a service rather than a product. This is indicated by a small SM next to the mark.

Spec Work is work performed in speculation of receiving a project and is done when several graphic designers are asked to submit free designs with their proposal. The American Institute of Graphic Arts and the Graphic Design Trade Customs are strictly against this practice, and the majority of designers will refuse to do spec work. Companies who want multiple design choices will often offer a fee to several design firms, but design contests other than for charity are considered speculative.

Statement is a summary of your company's account with a supplier. A statement shows your outstanding balance, often by thirty-day aging stages. It is not an invoice, but will list invoices already sent to you.

Terms are the number of days after which a supplier expects full payment for goods or services. Thirty days is usually the length of the term. Interest may be charged after thirty days, in the same way a credit card company would charge your personal account.

Thirty Days Net means complete payment in thirty days. It does not mean installment payments or other extended terms.

Trademark is the term used when the logo or logotype represents a product not a service. This is shown by a small TM next to the mark.

Transmittal Letter or **Letter of Transmittal** is a note or letter stating something has been sent from one company to another. If it is a package coming to you, the transmittal letter will tell you what you should be getting, and the sender will retain a copy of the letter for their protection. This is an excellent device for you to use as well.

CHAPTER 15

GRAPHIC ARTS TERMS COMMONLY USED

The following terms and definitions have been compiled to aid you in communicating with other graphic arts professionals. These definitions have been updated to include terms used in the electronic design, prepress and printing processes.

To list all of the terms used in the field of graphic arts would be counter-productive. Many are either too technical or have little meaning in your areas of responsibility. These are basic terms which are necessary for memos, proposals, RFQs, BPOs, POs, and contracts.

AAs are author's alterations. These are changes made to the copy by the author, and are considered billable to you the client.

Absorption is the rate at which paper takes liquid such as ink. It is also the rate at which light is transmitted through a translucent surface.

Accordion Fold is used to describe a brochure, pamphlet, etc., with two or more parallel folds resulting in an accordion-like format.

Additive Color is the term used when describing the combination of the pure colors of red, green, and blue. When combined electronically they produce white or are totally transparent. RGB is the acronym for these colors and generally refers to transmitted color, such as that seen on a computer monitor or television screen.

Against the grain describes paper that is folded at a ninety degree angle of the direction of its grain. This is usually considered the least acceptable way to fold a sheet, because it often causes cracking.

Airbrush is a way of applying color with a spray. It also defines an effect simulated electronically to give something a soft edge or a graduation of tone.

Analog Color is color that is transmitted in a non-digital manner. In printing, it refers to a color proof pulled from conventional separations.

Antique Finish is a natural rough finish of certain printing papers.

Aperture is the opening of a camera lens. The f/stop number signifies the size of the lens opening.

Art or **Artwork** refers to a mechanical or components of a mechanical to be photographed for the creation of a negative for printing. The new electronic technology refers to a prepress disk as a mechanical.

Ascender is the part of a lower-case letter that is raised in a line of type, such as the back of an *h*.

ASCII (Pronounced "Askee") is the American Standard Code for Information Interchange. This is a general standard for information processed as text characters, usually electronically.

Backbone is the back spine of a hard-bound or perfect-bound book.

Backing Up is the printing of the reverse side of a sheet printed earlier.

Bad Break in typography is any line that ends with a widow or begins with an orphan. (See *Widow* and *Orphan* definitions)

Basis Weight is the weight in pounds of 500 sheets of paper in a standard size for a printing press. 500 sheets of 60 lb text that measures 25" x 38" has a basis weight of sixty pounds.

Bit, in computer terminology, is a single unit of numerical information. The word is derived from BI*nary digi*T.

Bit Map, in computer terminology, is the complete image or page with all information portrayed by pixels.

Black Printer is the black in four color printing. It is the *K* in CMYK (cyan-magenta-yellow-black) notations.

Blanket is the rubber-surfaced roller on an offset press that receives the ink from the printing plate and transfers it to a sheet of paper.

Bleed is when an image, photograph, or area of color seems to run off the edge of a printed page.

Blind Embossing is the printing process where an image is raised on a sheet of paper through the use of dies, without color.

Blueline is a proof made with photosensitized paper from the final offset negatives that will be used to make the final printing plates. The color of the exposed area is blue.

Body Copy is the main portion of text in a printed piece. This in contrast to "Heads" and "Subheads."

Bold Face is the term used to describe type heavier in weight than the normal strength of its text face.

Bond is a grade of writing paper, used for letters and forms which generally comes in a 17" x 22" sheet size.

Book Paper may be coated or uncoated and is usually comes in a 25" x 38" sheet.

Break for Color is the keying of elements and areas for their assigned colors in printing. These can be screens, solids, or process builds. These are also called *color breaks.*

Brochure is generally any printed promotion that is more than two pages. A brochure can be as simple as a four panel 4" x 9" pamphlet, or an elaborate sixty-four page 8.5" x 11" full-color corporate capabilities promotion. Generally, a two page (front and back) promotion is considered a *flyer.*

Bulk refers to thickness of paper. This is often adjusted in book printing to give the desired thickness to the final printed product.

Burn is the term used when a printing negative is placed on photosensitized paper or a blank printing plate and is exposed to light to form a proof or a printing plate.

Byte is a single unit of digital information within a computerized image.

CAD-CAM is Computer Assisted Design and Computer Assisted Manufacturing.

Calender is the machine that gives smoothness and gloss to a sheet of paper at the end of the paper-making process.

Caliper is the thickness of paper, usually measured in the thousandths of an inch, called *Mils.*

Camera-Ready Art (CRA) means that copy is ready to be photographed to make negatives for offset printing.

Caps are capital letters. Hence, *all-caps* means all capital letters. The chapter titles in this book are set in all-caps.

Cast Coated is a paper which has been coated so that ink will stand up on the surface and offer the best representation of color. Most paper companies keep their coating processes secret.

CD-ROM stands for Compact Disk-Read Only Memory. The CD is just like your stereo CD, but works with graphic images instead of music. ROM means you can read the information on the disk, but you can't record on it.

Character is one letter or a symbol in a typeface.

CMYK is cyan, magenta, yellow and *K* for black. These are the ink colors used in four-color process printing. They are subtractive colors, as all four combined make black.

Coated Paper is paper that has received a coating of some kind in the manufacturing stage. These papers can be made in any color and can be dull or glossy. Ink generally stands up extremely well on this type of paper, which makes these papers a favorite among graphic designers.

Collate is to arrange of multiple sheets or pages in their correct order.

Color Balance is the correct relationship of the four process colors.

Color Correction is any method used to correct an imbalance of color in a printing image. Formerly dot-etching was often used to change the structure of a color subject by hand-altering the density or number of dots in a given area. Now, color corrections can be made electronically on the computer. Remember, the worst time to color correct is on press.

Color Keys are clear color overlays (usually made by 3M) to proof color breaks.

Color Proofs are representations of any color images or full color images, that let you see the effect of the colors that have been specified.

Color Separation is the division of each of the four process colors into their respective percentages that, combined, make up a full-color image or picture.

Condensed Type is a compressed letter form which occupies less area than the normal letter forms.

Contacts are photographic prints made by negatives directly exposed to photosensitized paper.

Continuous Tone is a photograph that has no dot structure. This is the opposite of a halftone.

Copy is material you furnish to a graphic designer or a printer and may include illustrations as well as text.

Cromalin is a color proof using the DuPont Cromalin process.

Crop is the term used to size and shape photographs or illustrations for reproduction.

CRT is a Cathode Ray Tube on a computer monitor, which is the monochromatic or color video display.

Curl is the effect caused by the differences of coatings on the two sides of paper.

Cut-Off is the print length of a sheet of paper on a web press or a paper machine.

Cyan is process blue, one of the four basic colors in four-color process printing.

Dandy Roll is a cylinder that creates a watermark in a sheet of paper during the paper-making process.

Deckle Edge is the edge of a sheet of paper that has been created to look torn or ragged. This effect is used on formal invitations and specialty printing projects.

Densitometer is an instrument that measures the density of printing ink on paper.

Descender is the part of a lower case letter that extends below the the rest of the characters such as the back of a lower-case letter *p*. This is the opposite of an ascender.

Die Cutting is a process by which a shape is cut through a piece of paper or board by the use of a die. The die, which resembles a sharp cookie cutter, can be used to create special folders or shapes.

Digital Color Proofs are produced from digital data. Conventional proofs need film; whereas digital proofs utilize digital information generated from a computer.

Digital Plates are generated, without negatives, directly from an electronic prepress system.

Digital Printing is plateless printing through electronic prepress. The process is used very effectively for on-demand four-color printing.

Dimensional Stability is the ability of paper or film to maintain its size and shape during changes in the moisture content and humidity within its environment.

Display Type is type used for headlines. It is set larger than other text within in the same area.

Dot is the smallest area of density in a halftone. If you look at any printed black-and-white picture (preferably in a newspaper because the screen is so coarse) with a magnifying glass, you will see the dots that make up the picture. The further away, the more the dots blend, making the picture look like continious tone.

Dot Etching is a way of altering a four-color image by using chemicals to eliminate or increase dots on the negatives or positives for any of the color in certain areas.

Dot Gain occurs when the dots in printing become larger and cause the ink to reproduce darker or more intensely than it should.

Dots Per Inch or "dpi" is the measure of how many electronic dots per inch are generated by a computer-linked printer. The more dots per inch, the sharper and crisper the image will be.

Draw Down is the process of spreading ink on a sheet of paper by hand, with a spatula, to test color.

Dummy is a bound replica of a planned printed piece. A dummy can be just a folded and stapled sample made up of plain paper, or it can be a complete bound proof.

Duotone is a process of giving a black-and-white photographs a two-color look. Consult your printer on the various duotone effects available. There is also a Pantone Matching System book available in art-supply stores.

Duplex Stock is paper that has two different sheets laminated together, so a different color or finish is on each side.

Dye Transfer is a photographic process for intensifying color and retouching photographs through the use of dyes. This process has been replaced by electronic retouching.

Electronic Dot Generation or **EDG** is the method for creating halftones electronically.

Em is a measurement in typography representing the space an *M* occupies.

Emulsion Side is the treated side of film that collects light causing a photographic image to appear.

En is a measurement in typography representing the space an *N* occupies, or half an Em space.

Enamel is the term used for the coating on certain gloss papers.

EPS (Encapsulated PostScript File) is a picture file format that allows PostScript information to be transferred between computers systems. EPS files are limited in the way they can be manipulated. The image can be scaled but it can only be ujsed in black and white.

Expanded Type is a typeface that is set wider than the normal version was designed.

Felt Side is the smoother side of a sheet of paper. It is generally the top of the sheet when it's being manufactured.

Flat is film ready to be converted into an offset printing plate.

Flatbed Scanner is a four-color scanner that scans an image flat, in contrast to wrapping the original around a drum.

Flush Left Ragged Right is the term for type that is not justified on the right side.

Folio is a page number.

Font is a specific typeface or type style.

Fountain is the area that adds water or synthetic gum to one of the printing cylinders on a printing press.

Front-End System, in electronic prepress, is the desktop area in the production and printing process

Galley Proof is running type before it is made into pages. Galleys are usually associated with older typesetting methods or book production. Computerized design systems bypass this stage and give the reader complete pages.

Gathering, in print binding, is the assembly of folded signatures in their correct sequence.

GCR is the Gray Component Replacement. All colors have a gray equivalent. Think of all of the colors in a black and white movie that are now gray.

Generation is each stage beyond the original in the reproduction process of an image that is either text or illustrative material.

Gigabyte (GB) is one-billion bytes.

Grain is the direction of the fibers within a sheet of paper. Folding against the grain can cause cracking. Grain *long* or *short* means which way the grain is running in a sheet.

Grayscale is the range of gray measured from white to black.

Gripper is the part of a printing press that holds and moves a sheet of paper.

Gumming is part of the plate-making process. Gum is applied to the areas on a printing plate that will not take ink.

Gutter is the inner margin of a bound publication.

Hairline is the thinnest rule possible that will hold up in the printing process.

Halftone is the reproduction of a continuous-tone image

screened so that dots are formed and the image can be printed as line.

Hardcopy is any visual material that is not on a computer screen, such as a manuscript, laser proof, or photocopy.

Hardware is the physical computer equipment, as opposed to software, which is information that operates the equipment.

Hickeys are spots where ink does not adhere to the paper surface during the printing process.

Highlight is the lightest area in a halftone, containing the fewest dots.

Holdout is the property within a sheet of paper which lets the ink set up and gives the richest color. Too much holdout can cause problems when one sheet's ink rubs off on another. This is called off-setting.

HSV is Hue, Saturation, and Value. This describes the luminance in computer graphic programs.

Hue is pure color, versus a tint or a shade. Tints of color have white added to them. Shades of color have black added to them.

Imagesetter is a device used to output paper or film from electronically-generated information.

Imposition is the order or position of pages on a printing form that will make up the correct signatures when bound and trimmed.

Impression, in printing, is the term for each time the printing press comes in contact with a sheet of paper.

Insert is a separate sheet of paper blown in or bound into a publication.

Italic is type that slants right and is the opposite of oblique. Oblique type slants to the left.

Justify, in typography, describes text that is both flush left and flush right. This book's text is justified.

Kerning, in typography, is the decreasing of the space between letters.

Keyboard is the unit containing keys on a computer. To keyboard copy is to type text into the computer.

Keyline is an outline indicating color breaks and other information for the prepress process.

Kiss Impression is the lightest impression possible to leave an image, in the printing process.

Kraft is paper or board made from unbleached pulp, usually tan in color.

Laid Paper is made with a pattern of parallel lines in the sheets, such as a ribbed effect. These papers have a specific personality and are used to achieve a specific look.

Lamination is a process in which heat is used to apply a plastic film to a printed sheet of paper. This makes the sheet more durable and colors appear more vivid.

Laser stands for Light Amplification by Stimulated Emission of Radiation. In prepress, lasers are used to produce images from digital data.

Layout is a graphic design term used for a prototype showing color and typographical relationships. In printing a layout is the format of the pages.

Leaders are the dots in rows, as in tabular materials. Leaders lead the eye across the page as in a table of contents or an index. These are also called *leader dots.*

Leading in typesetting is the space between lines of text.

Letterspacing is the opposite of kerning. Letterspacing is increasing the space between letters.

Line Copy is copy that does not need a screen to be reproduced. A line-drawing is an illustration that is made up of black and white areas only.

Local Area Network (LAN) is the linking of computer equipment. In the prepress area, it is the connecting of workstations and other peripheral equipment such as scanners and printers.

Logo or Logotype is the symbol or stylized word designed to identify an organization, product, or service. Logos are the symbols. Logotypes are the stylized words or names. A company can have a logo and logotype. For example, Johnson's Wax uses a stylized *J* for its logo, and spells out its name in a unique typestyle as its logotype.

Lower Case is the opposite of capital letters or "Caps." The word *case* comes from the compartmented wood boxes in which these letters were stored when type was set by hand. *Commoncase* is type that is designed to use upper and lower case letters in the same sizes and weights.

M is the abbreviation for 1,000 in the measurement of paper quantities or printed copies.

Magenta is process red. The color is a pinkish hue and does not look like traditional red.

Make-Ready is the process of setting up a printing press for a run. Inferior sheets are run through the press to get the color balanced. These are called make-ready sheets.

Matte Finish in paper means a dull surface. This is the opposite of glossy.

Measure is the width of a line of text in typesetting, usually calculated in picas.

Megabyte (MB) is the term for one million bytes. Disk capacity and RAM are usually measured in megabytes.

Menu is the computer term for choices of functions offered on the computer monitor.

Modem (MO*dulator*/DEM*odulator*) is equipment used to send information over phone lines from one electronic system to another. It converts data into high-frequency signals and vice-versa.

Moire is an undesirable pattern created when screen angles are incorrect. The pattern often appears as a plaid in a photograph, and is often the result of a printer screening a photo that was printed earlier..

Monitor is a computer video screen.

Mouse is a device that lets the computer operator move the cursor around on the screen by sliding a hand-held unit over a pad.

Mylar is a polyester film used in stripping. It has great strength and is very stable.

Negative is a piece of film with reversed images produced from a conventional camera or an imagesetter, and is used to produce a printing plate.

Newsprint is the type of paper used in the printing of newspapers. Made from ground wood pulp, it is inexpensive when compared to most grades of commercial printing papers.

Oblong is the term used for a booklet or publication bound on the shorter side.

OCR is Optical Character Reader. As the name implies, OCR converts/reads written or printed text and turns it into digital information for the computer.

Off-Loading, or removal of data from a computer, is usually performed when there is a need for more memory. This is also called "downloading."

Offset is the lithographic printing process, whose name derives from the fact the offset printing plate never touches the paper. An intermediate roller or blanket receives the image from the plate and transfers it to the paper.

Opacity is the opposite of transparent or translucent. It is the quality of paper to hide show-through, so that you don't see the images on the other side of the sheet.

Opaque is the process of covering areas on an offset negative to prevent exposure in non-print areas.

Overlay is usually a transparent material covering mechanical artwork, used for marking corrections, color breaks, or variable print runs.

Overrun is the number of copies printed in excess of the number ordered. Underrun, or shortage of copies, is the opposite.

Overset is the amount of text in excess of the space allotted for it.

Page is one side of one half of a sheet of paper in a printed piece. If you pull the center out of a saddle-stitched magazine, you will be holding four pages.

Page Makeup is the assembly of all of the elements that

represent a page. These elements can be illustrations, photographs, charts, graphs, typography, etc.

Palette is a group of colors available in a given medium.

Paste-up is the preparing of a conventional mechanical. The term comes from the era when rubber cement was used to literally glue type and other elements down on illustration board. Even with the advent of waxers, these mechanicals were still referred to as paste-ups.

Perfecting Press prints both sides of a sheet of paper with one pass through the printing press.

Phototypesetting is type set through photography. This is also known as "cold type," in contrast to the linotype method, called "hot type."

Pica is a printing measurement representing approximately one sixth of an inch. The pica measurements are used extensively in typesetting and page geometry.

Picking is the lifting of the printing paper's surface due to the tack of the ink. This occurs when the tack of the ink is stronger than the surface of the sheet.

Pin Register is the use of pegs/pins to align film, negatives, plates, etc. for perfect registration.

Plate is the name of the material carrying the image to be printed. Plates can be paper, plastic, metal, etc.

Point is a printer's measurement. There are twelve points in a pica, or seventy-two points in an inch. The height of type is always measured in points.

Positive is the opposite of a negative. The light and dark areas are the same as the original image.

PostScript is a computer language connecting different programs as well as platforms.

Press Proof is a proof pulled from running a color subject on a full-color press. This is an expensive way to proof a job, but the new electronic proofing systems are making press proofs less and less necessary.

Process Colors are the four colors used to achieve full-color printing. They're cyan, magenta, yellow, and black (CMYK). These colors are subtractive; when printed full strength over one another, they form black.

Progressive Proofs are made from the process color builds and show the sequence they will run when on press.

Ragged Left or *Rag Left* is the term used to describe type that is not justified on the left side.

Ragged Right or *Rag Right* is the term used to describe type that is not justified on the right side.

Raster Image Processor (RIP) is the processor that reads and converts copy into digital data to be utilized as graphics in a computer system. The term *ripping* is used in describing this process.

Ream is 500 sheets of paper.

Reflective Copy is any copy to be photographed that isn't transparent. Reflective copy can be scanned into a computer without being photographed.

Registration is the matching of images to make up a perfect unit. Registration marks are the guides used to correctly place one element over another.

Resolution is the measurement, in dots per inch (DPI), of paper or film output. The more dots per inch, the better the resolution, and the sharper the output. 300 DPI is considered low resolution, while 1200 DPI generally represents the beginning of reproduction quality resolution.

RGB are red, green, and blue, the primary colors utilized by video/computer monitors. These are additive colors. When they are combined in their full values, white is the result. This is the opposite of process colors, which form black when combined in full strength.

Run-Around is a term describing type that literally runs around a picture, illustration, etc.

Running Head is a headline or title at the top of each page in a publication.

Saddle Stitched is the wire binding method of stitching a booklet. The booklet/publication literally straddles a wire like a saddle and is stapled to hold it together. This is the opposite of perfect bound, where the pages are glued into the booklet and there is a spine.

Scaling is the enlargement or reduction of a graphic element to fit in a specific area.

Scanner is an electronic device that turns a graphic image into digital information to be manipulated by a computer.

Score is to make an impression in a sheet of paper so that cracking when folding is minimized.

Screen is a printing term describing the maximum number of dots in one square inch. A 65-line screen is recommended for newspaper reproduction because it is coarse, and will work better with the high absorbency of newsprint. A 200-line screen should only be used with a fine printing paper. The normal screen used by most commercial printers is a 150-line screen.

SCSI (*Pronounced Scuzzie*) means Small Computer System Interface. SCSI ports are connecting points on a computer for peripherals.

Self Cover means that the paper used for the cover of a pamphlet/publication is the same stock as the text. The opposite is *Plus Cover*, which signifies that the cover stock is different from the text stock.

Serif is the term used for typefaces with thick and thin strokes. The serifs are thin lines, or *feet*, appearing at the tops and bottoms of letters. The opposite of serif type is sans serif (or lack of serif). The letter forms within these type faces are plain and the weights are equal. The typeface used here is serif.

Sheetwise means running one side of a sheet of paper through a press, then turning it over and running the other side with a plate change.

Show-through is the opposite of opaque. This is when the images on the reverse side of a sheet can be seen through it, which is usually undesirable.

Signature is the term describing a printed sheet when it has been folded. Signatures are normally sixteen pages because eight pages can be printed on one side of a 25" x 38" sheet.

Silhouette means that a graphic element has had its background removed and appears to float on the page.

Skid is a wooden platform or palette holding paper or printed pages. Skids are used because they hold large quantities and can be easily moved by a fork-lift.

Small Caps are capital letters that are no higher than the main body of a lower case letter (SMALL CAPS).

Spiral Binding can be wire or plastic, and is a spiral as the name implies.

Step and Repeat is the process of duplicating pages.

Stet means disregard the changes indicated. This proofreading term is used when the proofreader decides something marked should return to its original state.

Stripping is the positioning of offset negatives for use in creating a plate, as done on conventional prepress.

Surprint means overprint. An example is a yellow box with black type surprinting over it.

Tagged Image File Format (TIFF) is the method for exchanging scanned images between applications.

Text is the body copy within a document, versus the headlines or sub-heads.

Thermal Printers produce color proofs, using a transfer sheet and heat to transfer images onto a page.

Tints are screen percentages of a solid color.

Tooth is a term used to describe the rough finish of a printing paper.

Varnish is used to enhance a printed image. Gloss varnish will brighten an image, while a dull varnish will mute it. Varnish is also used to make dark ink less likely to show fingerprints. Special effects can be achieved when tints of ink are added to a varnish. If you are going to flood varnish solid ink coverage on a sheet, and you are using a matte or gloss sheet, the paper surface will lose its identity.

Washup is the cleaning of a printing press (the rollers, fountains, etc.), preparatory to the next run.

Waterless Printing uses silicone coatings on the plates instead of water. This type of offset printing is environmentally friendly, as it doesn't produce pollution.

Web Press is a printing press that prints from rolls of paper rather than from sheets. Webs are used for long runs, providing economies of time and money for catalogs and other commercial publications.

Widow, in typography, is one hanging word, or partial word, at the end of a paragraph. This is considered undesirable by many, and you may want to rewrite the paragraph to delete the widow. An orphan is a column of type that starts with a widow at the top.

Wire-O-Binding is the same as spiral binding, but uses wire instead of plastic.

Wire side of a sheet of paper is the side opposite the felt side. The wire side is not as smooth as the felt side.

Work and Turn is the method of printing one side of a sheet and then turning it over from left to right and using the same plate to print the other side. This is ideal for short forms, because there is no wash-up between the printing of the two sides of the sheet.

WYSIWYG (pronounced Wizzie-wig) means "What You See Is What You Get." This applies to images on a computer monitor. Basically, what the screen shows is what the printer will output.

CHAPTER 16

THE GRAPHIC DESIGN TRADE CUSTOMS

Simply put, Trade Customs are the general terms and conditions for sales within the graphic design and printing industries. Trade Customs, however, are not contracts. They can always be circumvented in part or whole by an agreement between you, the client, and the designer or the printer.

The Graphic Design Trade Customs*

There have been many attempts at setting standards for the graphic design industry. The Graphic Artist's Guild has developed a Code of Ethics, which is meant to define the designer's responsibilities as well as the client's. These ethics are very good, and are in no way contradicted by the Trade Customs, which are aimed specifically at the business side of design.

In this section, I will explain what the Graphic Design Trade Customs mean to you as well as what they mean to the graphic designer.

---

*The Graphic Design Trade Customs are printed in their entirety on pages 164-167.

The American Institute of Graphic Arts (AIGA) has also published a Code of Ethics, as well as a standard contract for graphic designers. The problem with the AIGA contract is it covers so much detail, it can scare off a designer's potential client. This contract is viable for very large projects, I believe, but for the small to medium sized projects, the AIGA contract may be overkill.

Other graphic design professional organizations have published guidelines for writing contracts to protect the designer from all of the pitfalls a complicated project can produce. These guidelines are very helpful and should not be dismissed.

The bigger the bottom line, the more paper you need to cover it.

Contracts usually apply to one specific project, and further define the responsibilities of both parties, including scope of work, the schedule, the costs, and terms of payment. A contract is always a good idea. It may be no more than a letter of agreement between the client and the designer, but the rule of thumb is cover your bottom line. The bigger the bottom line, the more paper you need to cover it.

The Graphic Design Trade Customs define specific areas of responsibility between you and the designer. They lean toward protecting the designer, because you have a distinct advantage over the designer. It's the golden rule: "He who has the gold makes the rules." Without the Trade Customs, designers are sometimes at the mercy of their client's ideas and wishes.

Now that designers are in the "Electronic Age," there

seems to be a whole new set of problems concerning copyright and ownership of artwork. The Trade Customs address these issues with some very basic common sense. Unless there is another agreement between you and your designer, he owns the reproduction rights of his creations.

Be advised that the area of copyright ownership is a subtle one, yet because of recent changes in the law, it promises to be a controversial area which must be addressed. Ever watch the "Peoples Court" with Judge Wopner? It always seems that the party with a piece of paper wins. This is true in life and business as well. When you have established a solid paper trail, chances are you'll prevail in a common sense dispute. Of course that doesn't affect someone who is basically dishonest, but then again, nothing will.

Why do Designers and Printers have Trade Customs?

When you and a designer or a printer agree on the production of a work, you may not realize that the simple "contract" you sign carries a host of terms and conditions you neither intended nor realized were present. In almost every state there are laws grouped under a heading generically referred to as the Uniform Commercial Code (UCC). The code is a compilation of laws which address routine commercial transactions such as the formation of the agreement, the inclusion of terms and conditions, warranties which are made (or more often not made), and many other factors.

The UCC is intended to apply only to the sale of goods, but it is such a comprehensive work that courts tend to use it more widely, because it provides a relatively sound and predictable framework in which to solve any business disputes which might arise. While designers may well consider themselves in the service business, designers do in fact deliver a product or "good." As a result, the UCC could well be used (usually at the urging of a disgruntled client) to interpret the simple "contract" signed by designer and client. One example of the UCC's applicability to a standard "contract" could be the automatic inclusion of a warranty that the product is fit for the specific and particular purpose the client described to the designer.

While the UCC is not our focus here, it highlights the importance of crafting a clear statement of rights and responsibilities between designer and client and of clearly understanding the industry norm. When there is a dispute, the UCC guides a court in determining the rights and obligations of parties to an agreement. In cases where the parties have previously worked with each other, the court will look to this prior "course of dealing," to help determine what the parties knew and reasonably could have expected out of their relationship.

> *It pays the designer*
> *not to bury the trade Customs*
> *like some fine print in a*
> *real estate contract.*

If there is no track record, the court will look to "the standard usage of trade." In effect, the focus shifts from the particular parties, to what others in the industry do and have done in similar situations. It is the UCC's instruction to "look to the industry" which makes trade customs so important.

If an industry develops, harmonizes, and widely disseminates terms and conditions governing the dealings of its participants, it is only reasonable that a court look to these understandings for guidance in a particular dispute. It was with this understanding that the Trade Customs were drafted. The goal is to promote harmonious relations through well understood and clearly explained terms and conditions. Parties with knowledge of what is expected and obligated, as opposed to what is merely desired and sought, will always be better off, because the Trade Customs eliminate the confusion over terms which lies at the heart of so many simple business disputes. Therefore, in order to work with designers, you should understand the Trade Customs and their implications.

How and why were the Trade Customs developed?

The Trade Customs were developed for the International Design by Electronics Association. An earlier version was developed for the Art Directors Club of Metropolitan Washington and later edited to include the new technology.

The Trade Customs address responsibilities of both you and the designer, that are not spelled out in a commercial agreement between you. Any of the Trade Customs, which is altered by an agreement between you and designer, will no longer be in force. For example, some companies issue purchase orders to designers that contradict certain parts of the Trade Customs. If the designer does not formally disagree with your purchase order, you can rightfully claim that that Trade Custom does not apply. This is another good reason for the designer to make sure you have a copy of the Trade Customs as soon as possible.

What do the Trade Customs mean to me?

Let's look at each part of the Trade Customs and see what they mean to you, your company, and the designer. Some of these terms have been covered earlier in this book. They should now be read both for their part in the overall Trade Customs and for their relationships to one another.

1. *Estimates*

An estimate is a "best guess" as to what it will cost for the designer to produce a project. Estimates are usually offered when there are still some unknowns, but the designer needs to give you some idea for a budget. It is important for the designer to make it clear that the estimate is not a fixed-price bid or proposal, and to clearly spell out what elements are not included in the estimate. Common sense tells us there is no such thing as a "ball park estimate." The price a designer gives should be carefully thought out to cover the worst- case scenario, but since usually there are some unknowns, an estimate is an educated guess. I've learned that most people treat an estimate as though it's "carved in granite." Don't make this same mistake. An estimate is a *guesstimate*. A quote is just the opposite. Don't get the two mixed up.

2. *Quotation*

A quotation is a fixed price for producing a project. Generally, a quotation includes costs for all facets of the job. If there is any work not defined in the specifications, the designer should assign an hourly rate to this work and note it in the quotation as such. If any materials or out-of-pocket expenses, such as travel, food, lodging, etc., are not included, these areas should also be clearly stated in the quotation.

Quotations are subject to acceptance within thirty days, because the cost of labor and materials may change. This time frame can be altered if the you and the designer agree to change it. Quotations do not usually include author's alterations or changes by the client, because each company has a different approval process and a different way of organizing its work.

Sales tax is not included in a quotation unless the client and designer agree to include it. If your organization is tax exempt, you should furnish the designer with you tax ID.

3. Alterations

Alteration charges apply to changes you or your company make after the designer has produced the work initially agreed upon by both parties. The designer should make it very clear to you what constitutes alterations, such as how many layouts will be shown for what amount of money. The designer's concept of alterations may differ from yours, so the best course is for the designer to write a memorandum to you as to when alterations begin. It can be very dangerous and costly to try to explain these things later.

4. Overtime

Overtime, on the surface, seems very simple and straightforward. However, there are pitfalls. First, you should be informed if a change in the previously agreed upon schedule has made overtime necessary. Second, you should know what the designer's overtime rate is, and if at all possible, how much overtime will be needed. On the other hand, if overtime is contemplated from the beginning, let the designer know if this is part of your production requirements.

Overtime differs by designer. Some feel their hourly rate does not need to increase, because they work late hours on many projects anyway. Others feel that you should pay a premium for schedule changes that cause overtime.

5. Copyright/Ownership

The designer's work is automatically protected under federal copyright law. Until the designer agrees to transfer copyright ownership (as compared to merely handing over a copy of the work itself), the designer owns all copyrights to his or her work and decides what compensation he or she wants for the re-use of the work. Designers hold the rights to their work, even if you beat them to the copyright office and try to copyright their work for your company!

These principles also apply to designs produced electronically on a computer. Although a design is easy to re-use electronically, or even alter and then reproduce, the designer's rights remain the same. If a you issue a purchase order, prior to the start of a project, claiming it is your policy that all designs produced for your company belong to your company, the designer may have to relinquish his or her rights to the work if these conditions have been accepted and the client seeks a copyright assignment. If you issue a purchase order *after* the project is completed, the designers can determine if they wish to comply with these terms. If they decide not to comply, the Trade Customs are on their side.

6. Experimental Work

Experimental work, done by the designer at your request, is billable. If a designer develops a design for you without your authorization, the work is not billable unless you agree otherwise. This should not be confused with spec work, which is totally against the Trade Customs and most design codes of ethics. Experimental work is usually exempt from sales tax, as it is usually pure labor. It's best to find out if your state feels this work is taxable.

7. Condition of Copy

If you have stated that the final copy for a project will be submitted in a certain manner (such as on paper or disk) and the designer has given a quotation based on this information, the designer has the right to amend the quotation if you change these specifications. Similarly, if the scope of work has increased because the copy has changed in volume, the designer should amend the quotation. If you are aware that you have changed the specifications, you should ask for a cost update.

8. Production Schedules

Common sense dictates that production schedules established between you and the designer should not contain any liability factors for either of the parties if the schedule changes because of uncontrollable circumstances, or "acts of God." This can be superseded by a written contract with the designer.

If, on the other hand, the production schedule is delayed due to you or your company's review process, the time needed for the designer to complete the project should be increased in direct proportion to the extra time that you have used.

9. Client's Property

The designer should maintain adequate insurance to cover your property while in the designer's possession, unless that property is extraordinarily valuable. If your property is unusually valuable, it is your responsibility to notify the designer and to appropriately insure the property. The designer's liability cannot exceed the amount recoverable from the designer's insurance.

10. Outright Purchase vs. Reproduction Rights

Outright purchase gives you complete copyright ownership and re-use of the designer's work. This should be done in writing and worded very carefully, with specific work listed, to avoid later confusion about the extent and amount of work you purchased. It should be clear that the work can be altered, because of the widespread availability of electronic design and the use of high-end retouching work-stations.

Reproduction rights should be identified as to whether they are one-time or multiple usage rights. If there is no other agreement, one-time usage for a specific purpose is the Trade Custom. Again, it is common sense to clarify these terms.

11. Re-use and Extended Use of Artwork, Disks, or Negatives

Artwork, disks, or negatives should not to be re-used or adapted for other purposes without compensation or permission from the designer who created the original. Changing the artwork does not diminish the designer's ownership of it. If you want to re-use the work or change it, and you do not own all copyrights in the work, the designer who originated the work should be used. If the designer still owns the copyright and the artwork, disk, or negatives need updating, the original designer still owns the designs, and must authorize all further uses of the work.

12. Mark-ups

All of the designer's out-of-pocket or direct expenses are subject to a mark-up, or handling charge. Expenses subject to mark-ups include: photography, printing, illustration, advertising space, or special supplies/materials purchased for a specific project.

Mark-ups are handling fees and should discussed and agreed upon by you and the designer.

13. Speculation

Designers should not be asked to perform work on speculation. In a typical scenario, a client will ask three design firms or individuals to submit a design with a proposal. This might seem harmless on the surface, but if this becomes the rule and not the exception, two-thirds of the designers will be doing free work. The simplest answer is to remember that speculative work is against the Trade Customs. Offering a project overview within a proposal is not considered speculative work. It is more of a sign that the designer understands the project's scope and objectives.

14. Terms

As in any business, the designer should ask you for a purchase order prior to starting work. The purchase order should state the agreed-upon price, terms (such as net thirty days), and a production schedule.

If you cannot issue a purchase order, you should send a memorandum or letter of agreement detailing the same information that would be contained in the purchase order. You do not have to have the designer sign this letter if it says, "If any of the information contained in this (memo or letter) is incorrect, please notify (your name) in writing and/or by fax within twenty-four hours." Once again, a paper trail will protect you.

If you dispute the designer's invoice, Trade Customs states that your dispute should be made in writing and submitted to the designer within fifteen days after you receive the invoice. It is not uncommon for a designer's client to dispute an invoice when it is ninety days old and everyone's memory is a little foggy.

If there is a dispute over part of an invoice, you should remit the amount not in dispute within the terms of the designer's invoice, and handle the disputed portion as a separate item.

15. Liability

As printers specified in their own Trade Customs long ago,

the designer is only liable for the correction of his or her errors. It only makes sense, that because of the nature of technical jargon, whether it's medical, legal, or scientific, the ultimate proofing responsibility rests with you.

And, just as in the Typographers' Trade Customs, proofreading is your responsibility. Correcting an error is the designer's responsibility and should be done free of charge. In any case, however, the Graphic Design Trade Customs state that the designer is not liable for more than the design and production fees of a project.

If the designer is asked to approve a printer's proof because you cannot be available, the designer should have you sign a letter of agreement releasing him from any liability because of an error in proofing. If the designer is purchasing the printing and signs off on the printer's blueline, the designer may be liable if there is a mistake in the printed piece.

16. Indemnification

This somewhat intimidating word simply means that the designer is protected from liability if the designer unknowingly creates a design that is already in use, copyrighted, or trademarked. The key word is "unknowingly." Anyone can accidentally design something that is in use somewhere else (and this does not constitute copyright infringement). You have the responsibility (as well as the legal obligation) to institute a trademark search for any word or logo design; you should produce nothing with the new mark on it until a thorough search has been made.

You should also be sure that all materials furnished to the designer are free and clear of any copyright or trademark problems. If the you fail to obtain correct usage rights, you, not the designer, are liable.

If you or your company make false statements, plagiarize, or otherwise illegally tamper with any copy submitted to the designer, you, not the designer, are responsible for any legal repercussions, and you accept all liability.

17. Print Management / Press Inspections

If the designer offers to press inspect a project, your responsibility for final proofreading remains in effect, and you must sign off on the blueline. The designer is responsible only for signing off on a press proof that the color is acceptable by industry standards. The printer is responsible for ensuring that the remainder of the press run is consistent with the approved press proof.

You should be allowed to attend a press inspection, to offer a different perspective on proofing, and to participate in the final okay for color.

What Do the Trade Customs Really Mean?

The Graphic Design and Printing Trade Customs are terms and conditions of sales. They state what the design and printing industries consider common practice and specify how they do business. If your company's policies differ, it is best to get this out, up front.

The Graphic Design Trade Customs can vary from one design firm to another. It is important to read each set and look for the differences. As I mentioned earlier, these are just terms of conditions for sales, and you always have the right to issue your own terms. But this must be done up-front, not when the project is completed.

The Graphic Design Trade Customs are printed in their entirety on the following pages.

The Graphic Design Trade Customs

The Graphic Design Trade Customs were developed by the International Design by Electronics Association and the Art Director's Club of Metropolitan Washington.

Trade Customs are those practices which delineate the specific areas of responsibility with regard to a special trade or operation which might not be outlined in a commercial agreement. Where a commercial agreement is silent with regard to one or more practices, the Trade Customs areas are used to interpret the intent of the parties. It should be clearly understood that the Trade Customs protect both parties in a commercial agreement. It is, therefore, the responsibility and obligation of involved parties to understand their content and meaning.

1. Estimate: (A preliminary projection of cost which is not intended to be binding.) Estimates are based upon prevailing wages, the anticipated hours of work, and the cost of materials and supplies necessary to produce work in accordance with preliminary copy, style and specifications. They are not binding upon the designer unless a firm quotation has been issued.

2. Quotation: A quotation is a fixed price for producing a given project. A quotation is firm unless otherwise specified. Quotations are subject to acceptance within 30 days and are based on the cost of labor and materials on the date of the quote. If changes occur in the cost of materials, labor or other costs prior to acceptance, the right is reserved to change the price quotes. Subsequent projects will be subject to price revision if required. Quotations do not include alterations or applicable sales tax unless otherwise specified.

3. Alterations: Alteration charges are incurred by a client when a change is made to: approved layout, approved manuscript, mechanicals or disk produced correctly, or any new work not within the original specifications.

4. Overtime: Overtime is work performed by the designer in excess of the work schedule of the project. Overtime may be charged at the designer's prevailing rates for this service.

5. Copyright/Ownership: Creative work such as sketches, illustrations, layouts, designs, icons, logos, etc. produced on paper, computer disks or any other medium, are protected under the 1976 Copyright Act. Until the designer transfers ownership rights, creative work remains the property of the designer. There can be no use of the designer's work except upon compensation to be determined by the designer. Purchase orders issued after the completion of creative work, claiming the client's ownership of creative work, are not valid unless agreed upon by both parties.

6. Experimental Work: Experimental or preliminary work performed at the client's request will be charged at current rates, and may not be used by the client until the designer has been reimbursed in full for the work performed. All experimental work performed by a designer without authorization of the client is not billable.

7. Condition of Copy: If original copy, disk or manuscript, furnished by the client to the designer, differs from that which has been originally described and consequently quoted, the original quotation shall be amended or a new quotation will be issued.

8. Production Schedules: Production schedules will be established and adhered to by client and designer, provided that neither shall incur any liability or penalty for delays due to state of war, riot, civil disorder, fire, labor trouble, strikes, accidents, energy failure, equipment breakdown, delays of suppliers or carriers, action of government or civil authority, and acts of God or other causes beyond the control of client or designer. Where production schedules are not adhered to by the client, final delivery date(s) will be subject to renegotiation.

9. Client's Property: The designer will maintain fire, extended coverage, vandalism, malicious mischief, and sprinkler leakage insurance covering all property belonging to the client while such property is in designer's possession. The designer's liability for such property shall not exceed the amount recoverable from such insurance. Client's property of extraordinary value shall be specially protected only if the client identifies the property as requiring extraordinary coverage.

10. Outright Purchase vs. Reproduction Rights: These terms should be established at the time of purchase. Outright purchase gives the buyer physical possession of the artwork, disk or negatives, while reproduction rights and related copyright interests require the return of the original to the artist. Outright purchase does not give to the buyer commercial or private reproduction rights or any other copyright interests unless so stipulated in the purchase agreement. The matter of first reproduction rights with subsequent reproduction rights, subject to additional compensation, should be clearly understood at the time of purchase.

11. Re-use and Extended Use Of Artwork, Disk Or Negatives: Artwork disk or negatives purchased for a specific use cannot be re-used or adapted for other purposes than originally planned without additional compensation to the artist. If this possibility exists at the time of purchase, it should be so stated and the price adjusted accordingly. If re-use or adaptation occurs after purchase, the buyer should negotiate reasonable additional compensation with the artist. Whenever adaptation requires the services of an artist, and the creator has performed to the buyer's satisfaction, the same artist should be given the opportunity to revise his own work.

12. Mark-ups: Any services or goods such as typography, printing, photography, etc., or materials used specifically for the completion of a given project will be billed to the client with an appropriate mark-up. This mark-up is a handling fee only and unless otherwise agreed, does not include any professional or management fees.

13. Speculation: Graphic designs should not be asked for on speculation by a client. Design contests, except for educational or philanthropic purposes, are also considered speculation, and not a trade custom.

14. Terms: By assigning an order either verbally or in writing or by purchase order, the client agrees to the designer's terms of payment and late charges on unpaid balances prescribed to by the designer. Payment shall be whatever was set forth in quotation or invoice, unless otherwise provided in writing. Disputes over invoices must be made by the client in writing within a period of fifteen (15) days after the client's receipt of the invoice in question. Failure to make such claim within the stated period shall constitute acceptance, and an admission that the client agrees with the invoice submitted. If only a portion of the invoice is in dispute, it is the client's responsibility to pay the portion not in dispute within the terms of the invoice.

15. Liability: A designer is only liable for the correction of errors made during the design and mechanical processes. The ultimate proofing prior to printing is always the client's responsibility, unless the designer accepts this responsibility in written agreement. In any instance, the designer cannot be liable for more than the design and mechanical costs of a job in dispute.

16. Indemnification: The client shall indemnify and hold harmless the designer from any and all losses, costs, expenses, and damages (including court costs and reasonable attorney fees) on account of any and all manner of claims, demands, actions, and proceedings that may be instituted against the designer on grounds alleging that the said designer unknowingly violated any copyrights or any proprietary right of any person. Any materials such as photographs, photostats, transparencies, drawings, paintings, maps, diagrams, etc. furnished by the client to the designer should be free and clear of any copyright or trademark infringements. The designer is indemnified against any liability pursuant to the client's failure to obtain correct usage rights for said materials. Any false statements knowingly or unknowingly given to the designer, by the client, to be used as factual information to promote a product or service, shall remain the client's sole responsibility for substantiation. The designer is indemnified from any liability due to the client's negligence.

17. Print Management/Press Inspections: If a designer performs a press inspection for a client, the client's responsibility for proofing remains in effect. If the client has signed a printer's blueline, the designer is not responsible for any errors reflected in the approved blueline. If the designer approves color on a press proof or any other color proof, the designer is only responsible for approving color acceptable by industry standards. The printer is responsible for ensuring that the subsequent press run matches the color within acceptable standards of the proof approved by the designer.

I wrote the Trade Customs for the Art Directors Club of Metropolitan Washington D.C. in 1985. Later they were amended to reflect the electronic technology and adopted by the International Design by Electronics Association (IDEA). They were published in *Step By Step* magazine in the fall of 1992. Now they are part of the Graphic Artists Guild's *Collected Papers*.

The Graphic Design Trade Customs can vary from one design firm to another. It is important to read each set and look for the differences. As I mentioned earlier, these are just terms of conditions for sales and you always have the right to issue your own terms. But this must be done up-front, not when the project is completed.

CHAPTER 17

THE PRINTING INDUSTRY TRADE CUSTOMS

The Printing Trade Customs* are similar to the Graphic Design Trade Customs. They are usually printed on the reverse side of a printer's estimate sheet. If you receive a printer's estimate by fax, read the front to see if there is a reference to information printed on the reverse side. This is a good idea with any fax. Lease agreements almost always have terms printed on the reverse side.

The printing industry depends on the Trade Customs to ensure their position in areas of liability. You must read them and understand their magnitude. Printers usually have more at stake than graphic designers because of their overhead. For example, the cost of paper alone can be a large financial liability if a printing job is rejected.

The printing trade customs have been in existence for many, many years. They have been challenged in court, but they've always prevailed when they were properly presented to a customer. Most printers subscribe to the industry's standards but some have created their own.

---

*The Printing Trade Customs are printed in their entirety on pages 175-178.

You have rights

You can disagree with any portion of the Printing Trade Customs as long as you do it in advance and the printer agrees. Your best way to change the terms of the printer's Trade Customs is to state your own, and have the printer agree in writing. Remember, everything is negotiable and you are the printer's customer. I don't mean for you to be unreasonable, but you have just as much of a right to have your own terms.

Your purchase order can be your Trade Customs

You should always issue a purchase order (PO) when starting a printing project. And no project is too small.

On your purchase order, you should reference the way your company does business. If you feel, for instance, that the negatives or any materials generated by the printer, belong to you, it should be clearly stated on your PO. If you disagree with overruns and underruns, that should also be stated. The key phrase to making it work is this: "Upon acceptance of this purchase order, you (the printer) agree to my terms and conditions as stated within this written order."

Your company may be using purchase orders that are not specifically aimed at printing. If so, change them now.

Let's look at the Printing Trade Customs and what they mean in the areas of responsibility on your part, as well as the printer's. Once again, you will see these customs are weighted in the printer's favor. For your sake, now is the time to formulate your own set of rules to be incorporated in that new purchase order you're composing.

1. Quotation

A quotation is only good for sixty days. The quote is based on current material costs. Quotations can vary by what is included in the total price versus separate costs for halftones, color separations, etc. Make sure each quote gives a true bottom line.

2. Orders

Orders, verbal or written, cannot be cancelled without some compensation to the printer, if expenses have been incurred.

3. Experimental Work

Experimental work is work that you have requested and that the printer produced. Without compensation this work remains the printer's property. You should discuss this with the printer, up-front.

4. Creative Work

Creative work such as layouts, artwork, etc., all remain the property of the printer. If this is contrary to your wishes, I suggest you include an amendment to this custom in your , if you feel the creative work belongs to you or your company. Remember, everything is negotiable.

5. Condition of Copy

This parallels the Graphic Design Trade Customs inasmuch as the copy should be the same as what was quoted on. If it is manuscript, for example, it should be prepared in a clean, professional manner. If not, expect extra charges.

6. Preparatory Materials

Preparatory materials are treated the same as items 3 and 4. They are the property of the printer. Once again, you may want to revisit this in your purchase order. There is no reason why you or your company shouldn't retain the rights to your negatives.

7. Alterations

Alterations or change orders are billable. This is an area where you can control costs. Be aware that this is a profit center for most printers, because customers are often careless during the proofing stages. If you proofread meticulously, this is an area where you can definitely control costs.

8. Prepress Proofs

Prepress proofs are a printer's bible, and you must treat them the same way. Always make a photocopy of any proof you sign. If you mark "OK with corrections," it is still your responsibility to make sure the printer makes the corrections. In this age of fax machines, it should always be possible for you to sign-off one last time, so that the final printed piece has *your* approval.

9. Press Proofs

Press proofs are not usually included in the printer's estimate or quote. They are expensive and, for most jobs, unnecessary. You are usually welcome to press inspect your job at the time of make-ready.

10. Color Proofing

This provision simply gives the printer some wiggle room in matching color. It's up to you to ensure the quality of the work. Here again, the best solution is for you to be on site at the time your job is run.

11. Overruns and Underruns

Overruns and underruns may customarily be up to ten percent either way. If you must yield a certain number of copies, you may want to increase your order to ensure yourself of receiving the quantity you need. This is true, not only with printing, but also with specialty items like three-ring binders, cassette cases, etc. And with specialty items you will be charged for the overs. This can get tricky; so make sure you understand your agreement with your vendor before these items are produced.

12. Customers Property

This Custom is similar to that of the Graphic Design Trade Customs. It states that the printer will maintain reasonable insurance. If your property exceeds the amount recoverable from the printer's insurance, it's up to you to get more insurance. This is important, especially when it comes to paintings, photographs, or complicated electronic files that have been created by the printer.

13. Delivery

The printer will make local deliveries within the quoted price. If there are special delivery needs, these will be billed as a separate cost to you. The printer will keep accurate and reasonable records; you should do the same.

14. Production Schedules

Production schedules are a two-way street. The printer is not responsible for an interruption due to equipment failure, war, acts of God, or other typical, uncontrollable incidents that affect all of us.

15. Customer-Furnished Materials

This means that any materials you supply to the printer should be produced to the printer's specifications. If they are not, you will be billed accordingly. It is best to meet with the printer and designer to make sure everyone is on the same wave-length.

16. Terms

The printer requires total payment as set forth in the proposal, quote, or bid. If there is a dispute, it must be filed in writing within fifteen days of delivery of the printed job.

17. Liability

The printer is not liable for any amount exceeding the cost of the *printed job*. This covers profits lost by you or your company. Moreover, if you have not paid the printer for any past service, your work could be held hostage until you pay what's owed.

18. Indemnification

This frees the printer of any liability due to copyright infringements, untrue statements you have made in the copy, or just about any other mishap that is beyond the printer's control. With the volume most printers produce, this is a very fair arrangement.

The following pages present the Printing Trade Customs in their entirety. This is one version, and other printers may have modified versions. Please review these carefully, as I have only skimmed over them above, in an attempt to make them clearer.

As I mentioned earlier, the Printing Trade Customs can also vary from one printing company to another. It is important to read each set and look for the differences. These are just terms of conditions for sales. Remember, you always have the right to issue your own terms. But this must be done up-front, not when the project is completed.

The Printing Trade Customs

Trade Customs have been in general use in the Printing Industry through-out the United States of America for more than 60 years.

Originally formally promulgated, Annual Convention, United Typothetae of America, 1922. Revised and updated and repromulgated, Annual Convention, Printing Industries of America, Inc. 1945 and 1974.

1. Quotation: A quotation not accepted within sixty (60) days is subject to review. All prices are based on material costs at the time of quotation.

2. Orders: Orders regularly placed, verbal or written, cannot be cancelled except upon request that will compensate printer against loss incurred in reliance of that order.

3. Experimental Work: Experimental or preliminary work performed at the customer's request will be charged for at the current rates, and may not be used until the printer has been reimbursed in full for the amount of the charges.

4. Creative Work: Creative work such as sketches, copy, dummies, and all preparatory work developed and furnished by the printer, shall remain his exclusive property and no use of the same shall be made, nor any ideas obtained therefrom be used, except upon compensation to be determined by the printer, and not expressly identified and included in the selling price.

5. Condition of Copy: Upon receipt of original copy or manuscript, should it be evident that the condition of the copy differs from that which had been originally described and consequently quoted, the original quotation shall be rendered void and a new quotation issued. All original copy or manuscript should be clearly typed, double-spaced on 8.5" x 11" uncoated stock, one side only. Condition of copy which deviates from this standard is subject to re-estimating and pricing review by the printer at the time of submission of copy, unless otherwise specified in estimate.

6. Preparatory Materials: Working mechanical art, type, negatives, positives, flats, plates, and other items when supplied by the printer, shall remain his exclusive property unless otherwise agreed in writing.

7. Alterations: Alterations represent work performed in addition to the original specifications. Such additional work shall be charged at current rates, and be supported with documentation upon request.

8. Prepress Proofs: Prepress proofs shall be submitted with original copy. Corrections are to be made on "master set," returned marked "OK" or "OK with corrections," and signed by the customer. If revised proofs are desired, request must be made when proofs are returned. Printer cannot be held responsible for errors under any or all of the following conditions: if the work is printed per customer's OK; if changes are communicated verbally; if the customer has not ordered proofs; if the customer has failed to return proofs with indications of changes; or if the customer has instructed printer to proceed without submission of proofs.

9. Press proofs: Unless specifically provided in printer's quotation, press proofs will be charged for at current rates. An inspection sheet of any form can be submitted for customer approval, at no charge, provided customer is available at press during the time of make-ready. Lost press time due to customer delay, or customer changes and corrections, will be charged at current rates

10. Color Proofing: Because of differences in equipment, processing, proofing substrates, paper, inks, pigments, and other conditions between color proofing and production pressroom operations, a reasonable variation in color between color proofs, and the completed job shall constitute acceptable delivery.

11. Overruns And Underruns: Overruns or underruns not to exceed 10% on quantities ordered or the percentage agreed upon, shall constitute acceptable delivery. Printer will bill for actual quantity delivered within this tolerance. If the customer requires guaranteed exact quantities, the percentage tolerance must be doubled.

12. Customer's Property: The printer will maintain fire, extended coverage, vandalism, malicious mischief, and sprinkler leakage insurance on all property belonging to the customer, while such property is in the printer's possession; printer's liability for such property shall not exceed the amount recoverable from such insurance. Customer's property of extraordinary value shall be insured through mutual agreement.

13. Delivery: Unless otherwise specified, the price quoted is for single shipment, without storage, F.O.B. local customer's place of business or F.O.B. printer's platform for out-of-town customers. Proposals are based on continuous and uninterrupted delivery of complete order, unless specifications distinctly state otherwise. Charges related to delivery from the customer to the printer, or from customer's suppliers to the printer, are not included in any quotations unless specified. Special priority pickup or delivery service will be provided at current rates upon customer's request. Materials delivered from customer or his suppliers are verified with delivery ticket as to cartons, packages or items shown only. The accuracy of quantities indicated on such tickets cannot be verified, and printer cannot accept liability for the shortage based on supplier's tickets. Title for finished work shall pass to the customer upon delivery to carrier at shipping point or upon mailing of invoices for finished work, whichever occurs first.

14. Production Schedules: Production schedules will be established and adhered to by customer and printer, provided that neither shall incur any liability or penalty for delays due to state of war, riot, civil disorder, fire, labor trouble, strikes, accidents, energy failure, equipment breakdown, delays of suppliers or carriers, action of Government or civil authority, and acts of God or other causes beyond the control of customer or printer. Where production schedules are not adhered to by the customer, find-elivery date(s) will be subject to renegotiation.

15. Customer Furnished Materials: Paper stock, inks, camera copy, film, color separations, and other customer-furnished material shall be manufactured, packed, and delivered to printer's specifications. Additional costs due to delays or impaired production caused by specification deficiencies shall be charged to the customer.

16. Terms: Payment shall be whatever was set forth in the quotation or invoice, unless otherwise provided in writing. Claims for defects, damages or shortages must be in writing, and must be made by the customer in writing within a period of fifteen (15) days after delivery of all or any part of the order. Failure to make such claim within the stated period shall constitute irrevocable acceptance and an admission that they fully comply with terms, conditions and specifications.

17. Liability: Printer's liability shall be limited to stated selling price of any defective goods, and shall in no event include special or consequential damages, including profits (or profits lost). As a security for payment of any sum due or to become due under terms of any agreement, printer shall have the right, if necessary, to retain possession of and shall have a lien on all customer property in printer's possession' including work in process and finished work. The extension of credit or the acceptance of notes, trade acceptance, or guarantee of payment shall not affect such security interest and lien.

18. Indemnification: The customer shall indemnify and hold harmless the printer from any and all loss, cost, expense, and damages (including court costs and reasonable attorney fees) on account of any and all manner of claims, demands, actions, and proceedings that may be instituted against the printer on grounds alleging that the said printing violates any copyrights or any proprietary right of any person, or that it contains any matter that is libelous or obscene or scandalous, or invades any person's right to privacy or other personal rights, except to the extent that the printer contributed to the matter. The customer agrees, at the customer's own expense, to promptly defend and continue the defense of any such claim, demand, action or proceeding that may be brought against the printer, provided that the printer shall promptly notify the customer with respect thereto, and provided further that the printer shall give to the customer such reasonable time as the exigencies of the situation may permit in which to undertake and continue the defense thereof.

PROFESSIONAL ORGANIZATIONS AND PUBLICATIONS THAT CAN HELP YOU

There are many professional organizations that can help you achieve many things. Some of the benefits are: education, technical support, networking, new product and service information, conferences/seminars, or just social contacts.

This chapter also lists professional publications that can help you learn more about graphic design trends. There is also a listing of publications that will give you invaluable sources of graphic design, illustration, stock photography, and live photography.

Design Organizations Are Not Just for Designers

If you are involved with graphic design, you may wish to join the local art director's club in your area, which can give you an inside track on what's happening in that field. If you only want to attend certain meetings, featuring speakers you are interested in, you can find a designer who is a member and go as their guest.

Most people don't realize that you don't have to be a member of an organization to get on its mailing list. These groups welcome guests to their meetings. In fact, they promote it openly.

If you are a designer, joining a design group is even more important, because you can't afford to become insulated from the latest trends. If you're a design buyer, you'll be kept up to date by the designers you use.

Design organizations as well as other professional organizations, welcome allied members to join them. If you are involved indirectly with the design community, you will learn much from their organizations' seminars and conferences. Another important benefit is the ability to network. If you're buying design now, you could be selling it later. If you can't find a local design group, you can join the following organizations on a national level:

American Institute of Graphic Arts (AIGA)
164 Fifth Avenue
New York, NY 10010

(212) 807-1990

The AIGA is involved with the issues of design rather than with the designer. They publish monthly newsletters and hold conferences and seminars, and present an annual show of juried design work. AIGA has thirty-five chapters and approximately eighty-five-hundred members.

American Society of Media Photographers (ASMP)
Washington Park #502
13 Washington Road
Princeton Junction, NJ 08550

(609) 799-8300

ASMP is a professional organization of photographers. You don't need to join to attend informative meetings on issues ranging from copyrights to the latest techniques in photography.

Art Directors' Club of Los Angeles
1258 N. Highland, #209
Los Angeles, California

(213) 465-8707

ADLA has an annual show each year and they produce a catalog showing the winners. They are also involved in educational and social programs.

Art Directors' Club of Metropolitan Washington DC
1000 Eagles Passage Court
Davidsonville, MD 21035

(301) 261-4166

The Art Directors' Club of Metropolitan Washington DC is very active and its programs focus on the business side of graphic design. They hold an annual show, juried by nationally known designers in the "print" community.

Art Directors' Club of New York
250 Park Avenue South
New York, NY 10003

(212) 674-0500

The Art Directors' Club of New York is well known in the "print" community for its annual show. The club's board is made up of some of the greats in design.

Graphics Artists Guild
11 West 20th Street
New York, NY 10011

(212) 463-7730

The GAG was formed by artists for artists dedicated to protecting their rights and ethical standards. This group is geared to designers rather than buyers.

There are local chapters of these groups in cities across the United States. I suggest looking in your local phone book to see if there is one near you.

If you decide to join one of these organizations, it is important to remember that you only get out what you put in. This means your optimum return will be the result of working within the organization as a member of a committee. If, on the other hand, you're interested in networking or meeting peers, there are groups that easily afford this, such as the Jaycees, Rotary Clubs, or your industry's trade association.

Professional Publications are Valuable Tools

There are two kinds of publications listed in this chapter: magazines that inform you of current design and photographic trends, and source books on stock photography, live photography, illustration, and graphic design.

If you live in a metropolitan or a rural area, you will benefit from these publications. Many are free and once you are on their mailing list, you'll recieve them on a regular basis. Take advantage of the many free publications available to you as a buyer of design and printing.

Professional Publications of Graphic Design

Communication Arts Magazine(CA)
410 Sherman Avenue
PO Box 10300
Palo Alto, CA 94303

(415) 326-6040

Published bimonthly, in full color, and features the latest in graphic design trends. The magazine has annuals featuring the best in design and advertising.

Graphic Design USA
1556 Third Avenue
Suite 405
New York, NY 10128

(212) 534-5500

Graphic Design USA *is a monthly two color magazine giving the latest information on design and reporting who is doing what in the field.*

Graphis Magazine
1515 Broadway
New York, NY 10036

Graphis *is one of the the highest quality full-color publications of its kind, it features graphic design and photography from all over the world.*

HOW Magazine
P.O. Box 5250
Harlem, IA 51593-0750

1-800-333-1115

HOW *Magazine is a full color instructional publication offering design tips and techniques.* HOW *sponsors an annual a design conference.*

Print Magazine
104 Fifth Avenue
New York, NY 10011

(212) 463-0600

Print *Magazine is bimonthly and features the latest design trends. Printed in full color, with a regional issue each year, this an excellent publication.*

Step-By-Step
6000 North Forest Park
PO Box 1901 Drive
Peoria, IL 61656-1901

(309) 688-2300

Step-By-Step *is a full-color publication offering detailed information on design, illustration, and photographic techniques written by professionals in the field.*

Source Books for Finding Designers, Illustrators, and Photographers

This is a basic listing to get you started. There are plenty more and new ones are starting up all the time. These books highlight the work of the various designers, illustrators, and photographers, so that you can find the styles that appeal to you or are appropriate for a specific project.

Corporate Showcase
American Showcase
724 Fifth Avenue
New York, NY 10019

(212) 245-0981

This is an illustrated directory of designers, illustrators, and photographers. It shows their work and gives you their phone numbers.

Directory of Illustration and Design
PO Box 314
Brooklyn, NY 11205

(718) 857-9267

This full-color publication, showcases the work of illustrators, and designers from all over the US.

Stock Photography Catalogs

Allstock
222 Dexter Avenue N.
Seattle, WA 98109

(206) 622-6262

This catalog specializes in nature and wildlife photography. The images are mainstream and and typical nature shots as well as a mixture of other situations.

The Bettman Archive
902 Broadway
New York, NY 10010

There is nothing else as all encompassing as Bettman's extensive collection of classic photos, paintings, and other images.

Black Book Stock
Black Book Marketing Group
115 Fifth Avenue
New York, NY 10003

(212) 254-1330

This catalog features stock photography by various photographers with different specialities.

Comstock
Comstock Building
30 Irving Place
New York, NY 10003

1-800-225-2727

This catalog is more "middle of the road" with smiling faces and sunsets.

Direct Stock
10 East 21st Street
14th Floor
New York, NY 10010

(212) 979-6560

Direct Stock also features photography by various photographers, but with a little more flair.

FPG International
251 Park Avenue South
New York, NY 10010

(212) 777-4210

FPG contains stock photography much in the same vein as Comstock. It's very American, with nothing really experimental.

The Image Bank
111 Fifth Avenue
New York, NY 10211-0482

(212) 529-6700

The Image Bank is general stock photography and it also offers the latest in high-tech special effects.

Masterfile
415 Yonge Street, Suite 200
Toronto, Canada M5b 2E7

(416) 977-7267

Masterfile's catalog also features stock photography by various photographers with different specialities.

Photonica
141 Fifth Avenue, Suite 8 South
New York, NY 10010

(212) 505-9000

*Photonica has one of the most interesting collections
of stock images ever assembled. The photography is very
contemporary, and features images that are illustrations
in themselves. This book is the most radical departure
from the normal stock photography catalog I have ever seen.*

West Stock
2013 Fourth Avenue
Seattle, WA 98121
(206) 728 7726

*This is another general catalog featuring mainstream
stock photography by various photographers with
different specialities.*

References and Selected Readings

Berreswill, Joseph W. *Corporate Design/Graphic Identity Systems.* 1987, PBC International, Inc.

Black Book Marketing Group. *Black Book Stock.* 1993, H. Huntington Stehli (Publisher).

Committee, Editorial. *Graphic Artists's Guild Handbook, Pricing & Ethical Guidlines.* 1994, Graphic Artists Guild.

Crawford, Tad and Bruck, Eva Doman. *Business and Legal Forms for Graphic Designers.* 1990, Allworth Press.

Dejan, Daniel and Others. "Designers Guide to Print Production," *Step By Step.* February 1988.

Gold, Ed. *The Business of Graphic Design.* 1985, Watson Guptill.

Goodman, Danny. *Danny Goodman's Macintosh Handbook.* 1992, Bantam Books, Doubleday Dell Publishing.

Heron, Michal and MacTavish, David. *Pricing Photography: The Complete Guide to Assignment and Stock Prices.* 1993, Allworth Press.

Herring, Jerry and Fulton, Mark. *The Art & Business of Creative Self Promotion.* 1992, Watson-Guptil Publications.

International Paper. *Pocket Pal.* 1992, International Paper Company.

McQuiston, Liz, Kitts, Barry and Henrion, F.H.F. *Graphic Design Source Book.* 1987 Chartwell Books, Inc.

Pederson, Martin. *Graphis Corporate Identity.* 1989, Graphis Press Corp., Zurich (Switzerland).

Supon Design Group. *Using 1, 2 & 3 Colors.* 1992, Madison Square Press.

Sebastian, Liane. *Electronic Design and Publishing: Business Practices.* Allworth Press.

Wilson, Lee. *Make It Legal.* 1990, Allworth Press.

ABOUT THE AUTHOR

D on Sparkman is the president of his own graphic design firm, Sparkman + Associates, Inc. in Washington DC. He founded the company in 1973, and he has personally won numerous awards for design excellence, both nationally and internationally.

In 1976, Sparkman was selected the U.S. Bicentennial Committee as one of three designers to judge the design validity of all commemorative items developed for the committee.

He is a past-president of the Washington Metropolitan Art Directors Club and the International Design by Electronics Association (IDEA). He created the Graphic Design Trade Customs for IDEA, and has been published in *Step by Step* magazine. He has also lectured at the Design Management Institute's National Conference in Martha's Vineyard, George Washington University's Design Center in Washington DC, Northern Virginia Community College, the Corcoran School of Art, the American Institute of Graphic Arts, and many other institutions.

The Design & Printing Buyer's Survival Guide was conceived because of Sparkman's acute awareness of the problems encountered by buyers of print and graphics who have had no formal training. They may have little or no formal training, but their jobs are pretty risky, because what they produce is highly visible and can be held up to close scrutiny. Also, they often work with large budgets where it only takes one mistake to annihilate them. It is a question of survival which is one reason that smart buyers don't change suppliers when they've found ones they can trust. Sparkman has been on the other side for over thirty years, and he knows the tricks of the trade.

In order to keep providing excellent service, Sparkman has immersed his firm in the new technologies. In 1985 he bought a Lightspeed computer design system, which was one of the pioneer systems and very powerful for its time. Now, every designer in his firm works on a computer design system. On the other hand, Sparkman still believes that the computer is just another design tool, and that only people are designers. This philosophy has helped him keep his company on the leading edge of technology, while not forgetting why it is there.

INDEX

A

AAs, *131*
Absorption, *131*
Accordian Fold, *131*
Accounts Payable, *123*
Accounts Recievable, *124*
Additive Color, *131*
Adobe Illustrator, *31*
Against the Grain, *132*
Aging, *124*
Airbrush, *132*
Aldus Freehand, *31*
Alterations, *50, 60, 124, 126, 130, 158, 159, 166, 170, 174, 177*
Analog Color, *132*
Antique Finish, *132*
Art or Artwork, *132*
Aperture, *132*
Ascender, *132*
Arbitration, *124*
ASCII, *132*

B

Backbone, *132*
Backing Up, *132*
Bad Break, *133*
Basis Weight, *133*
Bit, *133*
Bit Map, *133*
Black Printer, *133*
Blanket, *133*
Bleed, *133*
Blind Embossing, *133*
Blueline, *124, 133*
Body Copy, *133*
Bold Face, *133*
Bond, *81, 134*
Book Paper, *81, 134*
BPA, or Blanket Purchase Agreement, *124*
BPO, or Blanket Purchase Order, *125*
Break for Color, *134*
Brochure, *134*
Brokering, *125*

Bulk, *134*
Burn, *134*
Byte, *134*

C

CAD-CAM, *134*
Calender, *134*
Caliper, *134*
Camera-Ready Art (CRA), *134*
Caps, *135*
Cast Coated, *135*
Cash Flow, *125*
CD-ROM, *135*
Change Orders, *125*
Character, *135*
CMYK, *135*
Coated Paper, *80, 135*
Cold Type, *20, 57*
Collate, *135*
Color Balance, *135*
Color Correction, *135*
Color Keys, *136*
Color Proofs, *136, 174*
Color Separation, *136*
Comp Time, *125*
Condensed Type, *136*
Contacts, *136*
Continious Tone, *136*
Contract, *125*
Copy, *136*
Cost Per M, *125*
Cromalin, *136*
Crop, *136*
Crosfield, *16*
CRT, *136*
Curl, *136*
Cut-Off, *136*
Cyan, *136*

D

Dandy Roll, *137*
Deckle Edge, *137*
Densitometer, *137*
Descender, *137*
Die Cutting, *137*
Digital Color Proofs, *137*
Digital Plates, *137*
Digital Printing, *137*
Dimensional Stability, *137*
Display Type, *137*
Dot, *137*
Dot Etching, *138*
Dot Gain, *138*
Dots Per Inch, *138*
Draw Down, *138*
Dummy, *138*
Duotone, *138*
Duplex Stock, *138*
Dupont, *16*
Dye Transfer, *138*

E

Electronic Dot Generation
  (EDG), *138*
Em, *139*
Emulsion Side, *139*
En, *139*
Enamel, *139*
Envelopes, *83, 84*
EPS, *139*
Estimate, *125, 158*
Expanded Type, *139*

F

Felt Side, *139*
Flat, *139*

Flatbed Scanner, *139*
Flush Left Ragged Right, *139*
FOB, Freight On Board, *126*
Folio, *139*
Font, *139*
Fountain, *139*
Front End System, *140*

G

Galley Proof, *140*
Gathering, *140*
GCR, *140*
Generation, *140*
Gigabyte, *140*
Grain, *140*
Grayscale, *140*
Gripper, *140*
Gumming, *140*
Gutter, *140*

H

Hairline, *140*
Halftone, *140*
Hardcopy, *141*
Hardware, *141*
Hickeys, *141*
Highlight, *141*
Holdout, *141*
Hot Type, *20*
HSV, *141*
Hue, *141*

I

Imagesetter, *22, 141*
IBM, *15, 17, 30, 31, 55, 58*
Imposition, *141*
Impression, *141*

Indemnification, 126, 179
Index, *81*
Insert, *141*
Invoice, *126*
Italic, *142*

J

Justification, *142*

K

Kerning, *142*
Keyboard, *142*
Keyline, *142*
Kiss Impression, *142*
Kraft, *142*

L

Laid Paper, *142*
Lamination, *142*
Laser, *142*
Layout, *142*
Leaders, *142*
Leading, *143*
Letter of Intent, *126*
Letterspacing, *142*
Liability, *126*
Line Copy, *143*
Lightspeed, *16*
Local Area Network (LAN), *143*
Logo or Logotype, *102, 103, 105, 143*
Lower Case, 143

M

M, *143*
Macintosh, *17, 58*
Magenta, *143*
Make-Ready, *143*
Mark-Up, *129*
Matte Finish, *144*
Measure, *144*
Megabyte, *144*
Menu, *144*
Microsoft Word, *17, 55*
Modem, *144*
Moire, *144*
Monitor, *144*
Mouse, *144*
Mylar, *144*

N

Negative, *144*
Newsprint, *144*

O

Oblong, *145*
OCR, *145*
Off-loading, *145*
Offset, *20, 22, 23, 81, 145*
Opacity, *145*
Opaque, *145*
Out Of Pocket Expenses, *127*
Output, *22*
Overlay, *145*
Overrun, *145, 172, 177*
Overset, *145*

P

Page, *145*

Page Makeup, *145*
Pagemaker, *31, 55*
Palette, *146*
Paste-up, *146*
Perfecting Press, *146*
PEs, *127*
Photo Art Direction, *127*
Photoshop, *31*
Phototypesetting, *146*
Pica, *146*
Picking, *146*
Pin Register, *146*
Plate, *146*
Pocket Pal, *7*
Point, *146*
Positive, *146*
PostScript, *147*
Press Proof, *147*
Print Manaagement, *127*
Printing Overrun, *127*
Printing Underrun, *128*
Proposal, *128*
Process Colors, *147*
Progressive Proofs, *147*
Purchase Order, *86-92, 124, 125, 128, 157, 160, 162, 163, 167, 168, 172, 173*

R

Ragged Left, *147*
Ragged Right, *147*
Raster Image Processor (RIP), *147*
Ream, *147*
Reflective Copy, *147*
Registered Trademark, *128*
Registration, *147*

Resolution, *147*
RFP, Request For Proposal,
  63, 66, 67, 68, 128, 104
RFQ, Request Fot Quotation,
  63, 87, 88, 89, 128, 130
RGB, *148*
Run-Around, *148*
Running Head, *148*

S
Saddle Stitched, *148*
Sans Serif, *45, 47*
Scaling, *148*
Scanner, *148*
Score, *148*
Screen, *148*
SCSI, *149*
Search, *128*
Self Cover, *149*
Serif, *45, 47, 149*
Service Bureau, *22*
Servicmark, *129*
Sheetwise, *149*
Show-through, *149*
Signature, *149*
Silhouette, *149*
Skid, *149*
Small Caps, *149*
Spec Work, *65, 129*
Spiral Binding, *150*
Statement, *129*
Step and Repeat, *150*
Stet, *150*
Stripping, *150*
Surprint, *150*
Syquist Disk, *60*

T
Tagged Image File Format,
  150
Terms, *123*
Text, *150*
Thermal Printers, *150*
Thirty Days Net, *129*
Tints, *150*
Tooth, *150*
Trademark, *129*
Transmittal Letter, *129*

V
Varnish, *150*

W
Washup, *150*
Waterless Printing, *151*
Web Press, *72, 151*
Widow, *151*
Wire-O-Binding, *151*
Wire Side, *151*
Word Perfect, *17, 55*
Work and Turn, *151*
WYSIWYG, *151*

ALLWORTH BOOKS

Pricing Photography: The Complete Guide to Assignment and Stock Prices by Michal Heron, 128 pages, softcover, ISBN 1-880559-11-0, $19.95

Electronic Design and Publishing: Business Practices, Second Edition, by Liane Sebastian, 144 pages, softcover, ISBN 1-880559-22-6, $19.95

Make It Legal: For Graphic Designers, Advertising Copywriters, Art Directors and Producers, Commercial Photographers and Illustrators by Lee Wilson, 272 pages, softcover, ISBN 0-927629-08-9, $18.95

Licensing Art and Design, Revised Edition, by Caryn Leland, 144 pages, softcover, ISBN 1-880559-27-7, $16.95

The Graphic Designer's Basic Guide to the Macintosh by Michael Meyerowitz and Sam Sanchez, 144 pages, soft cover, ISBN 0-927629-06-2, $19.95

Legal Guide for the Visual Artist, Third Edition, by Tad Crawford, 256 pages, softcover, ISBN 0-927629-11-9, $19.95

Business and Legal Forms for Graphic Designers by Tad Crawford and Eva Doman Bruck, 224 pages, softcover, ISBN 1-880559-26-9, $22.95

Business and Legal Forms for Authors and Self-Publishers by Tad Crawford, 176 pages, softcover, ISBN 0-927629-03-8, $14.95

Business and Legal Forms for Photographers by Tad Crawford 192 pages, softcover, ISBN 0-9607118-2-1, $18.95

Please write to request our free catalog. If you wish to order a book, send your check or money order to: Allworth Press, 10 East 23rd Street, Suite 400, New York, New York 10010. To pay for shipping and handling, include $5 for the first book ordered and $1 for each additional book ($10 plus $1 if the order is from Canada). New York State residents must add sales tax.